M000083619

Two Jeeps

Alex Kefford

Copyright © 2019 Alex Kefford. All rights reserved.
Photos on pages 2, 99, 150, 152 & 153 © Vince Bentley.
Jeep® is a registered trademark of FCA US LLC.
All other trademarks are acknowledged.

ISBN: 978-1095892282

No part of this book may be reproduced, stored, or transmitted, in any form or by any means, without the prior written permission of the author.

Also available as an e-book and audiobook.

This road-trip was climate neutral.

For bonus content including photos, maps and exclusive information about this trip, visit the Two Jeeps website:

www.twojeeps.com

CONTENTS

Chapter 1: London to Connecticut 5
Chapter 2: Connecticut to Philadelphia 15
Chapter 3: Philadelphia to Terre Haute. 33
Chapter 4: Terre Haute to Abilene. 43
Chapter 5: Abilene to Florence 57
Chapter 6: Florence to Moab. 67
Chapter 7: Moab 87
Chapter 8: Top of the World 101
Chapter 9: San Juan Skyway. 111
Chapter 10: Bryce Canyon. 129
Chapter 11: Capitol Reef 137
Chapter 12: Lockhart Basin. 143
Chapter 13: Steel Bender 149
Chapter 14: Canyonlands. 155
Chapter 15: Moab to Mexican Hat. 161
Chapter 16: Monument Valley to Las Vegas 169
Chapter 17: Las Vegas to California 187
Chapter 18: California to London 195

PROLOGUE

T HE GENESIS OF THIS TRIP stretches all the way back to 1997. I'd bought a Jeep® Wrangler and been consumed by the lifestyle that came with it. Before I knew what I was doing, I'd set up an organisation called JeepClub and was teaching people how to drive their Jeeps off-road without killing themselves or the environment.

That's how I met Vince. He and I formed one of those friendships that didn't have an identifiable start; it felt like we'd always known each other.

Vince fell into helping me run JeepClub almost by accident, and then tripped into a job at the same company I worked at. As a result, I think it's fair to say we know each other quite well.

Unfortunately, redundancy followed for both of us, and while Vince stayed in IT, I became a freelance journalist. As anyone who's been self-employed can tell you, it can quickly become all-consuming, and without realising I'd reached my thirties having achieved a lot for everyone else, but very little for myself.

I'd wanted to drive a camper van across America, stopping at as many national parks as I could, but that plan fell through – twice. So when Vince mentioned he had to be in Utah for a wedding, a plan began forming in our collective minds.

For Jeep owners there's one place on this planet that, more than any other, is begging to be explored. If owning a Jeep were considered a religion, Moab in Utah would be its Mecca.

The gateway to the massive red rock formations of Arches National Park, Moab boasts more off-road trails than almost anywhere else. Jeep enthusiasts are drawn from around the world by the chance to test their skills on trails such as Hell's Revenge, Steel Bender, and Metal Masher. In one day, you can drive from Helldorado to the Top of the World, with an emotional journey to match.

The Wrangler and Cherokee wait patiently behind bars at Southampton docks for their journey to begin.

But we didn't want to fly in and rent a Jeep like everyone else. We wanted to do something a little different, something that was 'once in a lifetime.'

"Why not take our Jeeps with us?" we thought.

So we hatched a plan.

We'd ship both our Wrangler and Cherokee across the pond to America so we could drive them where God (or at least Jeep) intended. But to ensure they were up to the challenge, they'd first spend a few weeks being extensively modified – suspension lifts, big tyres, winches, snorkels, etc.

With parts for Jeeps considerably cheaper in the US than they are in England, it didn't require much 'man maths' before the conclusion was drawn that it made sense to have the work done stateside. Our chosen engineering shop was based in Connecticut, making it convenient for the sea voyage to the port of New York. That just left us with the minor inconvenience of having to get two Jeeps across twelve states to Utah. And then, assuming we didn't break anything while we were there, crossing the remaining three states to catch our boat-ride home from LA.

Like all the best adventures it was high risk with many chances of failure. We had a limited amount of time available to us, the work on the Jeeps would take months, and we had to reach Utah on a date that couldn't be argued with.

For added flavour, I'd never driven in America – in fact, I'd never even been on a plane before – yet here we were, proposing a trip that would see us drive more than 2,500 miles in five days, 2,000 miles in the week that followed, and a further 1,200 miles to reach our ultimate destination on the west coast.

By the end of it Vince and I would need a holiday to recover, while the Jeeps would both need a service.

CHAPTER ONE

London to Connecticut

✈ + 00096⟲

I IMAGINE MANY OF THE greatest explorers in history have had their best-laid plans fall apart before taking the first step of a long journey.

Christopher Columbus, for example, set out in 1492 on the first of his great voyages to discover a route to the Indies. He'd estimated the distance at roughly 2,500 miles, only to realise they in fact lay rather inconsiderately 7,500 miles further out. Luckily for him fate intervened, and after five weeks he landed on what we now call the Bahamas.

In 1911, Scott of the Antarctic embarked on a quest to the South Pole equipped with a trio of freshly-invented snowmobiles. Even before the expedition had begun, one had fallen through the ice and sunk to the sea floor, while the remaining two broke down in the icy air.

I'm not about to suggest our trip registered on the same scale of importance to human history, but we too found ourselves at fate's mercy before we'd even left the airport. We were marooned in the departure lounge, unable to board the aircraft because the previous flight had broken down on the stand.

Our carefully choreographed itinerary didn't leave much room for manoeuvre. Its complex sequence of milestones had been painstakingly slotted together, like a particularly challenging game of Tetris, and each had to take place in order before we could move on to the next step. Perhaps this was fate's way of teaching us a lesson, but the need for flexibility was set to become something of a theme for the next few weeks.

After 9/11 airport security had become something of an elaborate pantomime. Performances ranged from the continual dance of removing one's belt and shoes so that they could be bombarded by x-rays, to the always entertaining game of trying to convince the check-in staff that your carry-on luggage didn't deserve to be banished to the hold.

My decision to carry my camera gear with me meant I soon became adept at re-attaching a lens, inserting a battery, and taking a picture of finest industrial-grade airport carpet to illustrate that it was, indeed, a camera.

This heightened state of security also meant that all US-bound departures had to be cleared by the American authorities before they could leave the gate, and on this day, having eventually made it on board the aircraft, it seemed our cousins in the colonies felt we deserved to sit on the tarmac for a little longer before finally earning their approval.

I ran through our itinerary in my head, trying to find areas where we could save a little time. There was so little room for manoeuvre – we had five days to get from Connecticut to Utah, a distance of more than 2,500 miles, and we couldn't be late. I slunk back in my seat, mentally totalling up the minutes. We were three hours behind schedule already, and with little chance of making it up. If only the Jeeps had been ready sooner, we could have left earlier and given ourselves more time, but an issue with the Wrangler's gearbox had developed from mildly annoying into full-on catastrophic failure. Securing and fitting a replacement had pushed our timeline somewhat closer to the wire than was comfortable.

Just as I was beginning to think our trip would end before it had even started, the captain announced the US authorities had decided we had by now paid our penance, and the aircraft was pushed back to begin its slow and ungainly trundle towards the runway.

As something of a petrol-head, anything to do with rampant acceleration is to be considered a good thing in my book. As we reached the edge of our allocated drag-strip the pilot wound up the four turbofans and restrained their howls against the brakes. It's possible I've seen *American Graffiti* too many times, but I peered out of the window as we sat there under starter's orders, half expecting to see a teenager drop a handkerchief to the ground. With that thought, the brakes were released and we began our express ride towards the horizon.

I chose this point in time, as one of Virgin Atlantic's most elderly of 747s struggled to hoist itself away from the Heathrow tarmac, to remind Vince that I had never flown before. Everything about this experience was new to me. Had it not been, I perhaps might have better understood the concern on Vince's face as the end of the runway drew ever closer yet without any apparent attempt at leaving it.

Of course the fact you're now reading a book about a road-trip and not a story of how a heavily-laden jumbo became embedded in the side of a hotel means we did at last claw our way into the crisp September air.

Eight hours later we landed at JFK New York and, along with 500 of our fellow passengers, began our weary trudge from the arrivals gate to immigration. Here, the very existence of our road-trip was to be threatened once again.

Our hike had delivered us to a large hall with imposing high ceilings, thick columns, and a floor space dominated by an elaborate queueing system constructed from crowd control barriers. At the far end border agents were restrained within numbered Perspex kiosks like rabid supermarket checkout operators, while above them hung a series of painted reliefs apparently depicting scenes from the five boroughs of New York City.

With an entire 747 disgorging its contents into this one hall, inevitably there was something of a wait to be processed. I shuffled my way through the winding forest of barriers while peering up at the murals in an attempt to discern their meaning. Fish markets, beach scenes, basketball players – it seemed hard to understand the common theme, but puzzling over this helped me at least divert my thinking away from the possibility of an unwelcome strip-search.

As I drew closer to the kiosks, I could see that the traveller ahead of me was receiving something of a dressing-down from the border agent. This culminated with a dismissive wave of his arm, signalling the man's rejection and the agent's desire for him to be banished from his presence. As the dejected man trudged away and with the agent's blood pressure now perilously high, he barked in my direction.

"You! Hurry up!"

Unaware of any delay longer than a millisecond, I left the safety of the 'do not cross' line and approached the kiosk.

"So have *you* bothered to fill out the waiver correctly!?"

UK citizens may travel to the USA under a framework dubbed the Visa Waiver Program which, as its name suggests, allows entry without formally applying for a Visa as long as certain conditions are met. Part of the process involves being handed a form to complete on the aircraft before landing, and while some questions are reasonable enough, others are a little ridiculous. "Are you now, or have you ever been, a member of a terrorist organisation?" It's hard to imagine under what circumstances anyone would tick the 'yes' box to that one.

Underneath the questions about whether or not I've ever been a Nazi is a section that begins "if you answered yes to any of the above..." As I'd answered no to each, my overloaded first-time-flyer brain had skipped an important question carefully concealed beneath.

Having inadvertently committed the same sin as the traveller before me, the border agent flew into a rage. To him, I might as well have been a Nazi. At least I would have ticked the box if I was.

"GO AWAY!" he screamed.

I picked up my waiver, retraced my steps through the maze of barriers, and found a member of staff willing to lend me a pen. I recounted my experience to her while correcting my heinous form-based transgression.

"It's the agent's job to get you through immigration. You are his responsibility, so please make sure you go back to the same agent when you're done," she told me.

My heart sank. I was hoping I could pick another kiosk, but unfortunately it seemed I had a date with 'cashier number four, please.'

I returned to my checkout of destiny and nervously held out my now perfected waiver. The border agent refused to take it. Instead he glared at it, sighed heavily, and let his hands drop to his sides.

Unable to decipher what this was supposed to signal, I gingerly placed the waiver on the counter, laid my passport next to it, and stepped back to allow him to choose which document to assess first. Shaking his head, he picked up the waiver and, without looking at it, placed it in a box beneath the counter. Next up, my passport. He examined the photo within and, while looking at the camera mounted to his left, said "look straight."

I looked straight at the camera.

"Look straight!" he screamed.

I began to realise the full force of Murphy's Law ("whatever can go wrong, will go wrong") was being visited upon my immigration experience. I turned my head and looked him squarely in the eye. He stared back, his face red with anger, for far longer than would be deemed 'uncomfortable.'

As he shoved my passport under the electronic reader he gestured to the fingerprint scanner. Placing my finger on the scanner elicited only a deep sigh from the agent. Clearly, I'd even done this wrong.

"Dab!" he instructed, pointing to a small, soft pad next to the scanner. These moistening pads are used to make the image of a fingerprint more distinct on the scanner but this one, I could feel, was bone dry. I didn't have the heart to tell him, and after two further attempts to take my fingerprint, I could almost hear the snapping of rubber gloves behind me. I was on the verge of being dragged into a back-room and ritually violated, and it appeared there was nothing I could do about it.

All patience clearly exhausted, the agent slammed my passport down on the counter, banged it with his fist for good measure and jerked a 'get lost' gesture over his shoulder with his thumb. I scraped my passport off the counter, what was left of my nerves off the floor, and hurried through the gate into the baggage hall, the border agent glaring at me all the while.

Vince was waiting with my bag by the carousel.

"Let's get out of here," I pleaded.

A customs officer was standing at the exit and, wincing at the prospect of another experience like the last one, I held out my customs declaration as I approached.

"Thank-you, sir, and welcome to America. I hope you enjoy your stay," he said as he took my declaration from me.

I nearly hugged him.

However, it seemed our trial-by-JFK-airport was not yet over.

I've seen TV programmes where architects talk at length about the need to create a smooth and logical passage through an airport to help move travellers quickly through the process and with as little stress as possible. Measures they enthuse about might include plentiful signage, bright and airy spaces, and clear sight lines from one end of a terminal to the other.

JFK had none of these things.

We had a simple mission: get to the Hertz car rental desk. Yet there were no signs, no maps, nor clues of any kind as to which direction we should take. We trudged about at random for some time, only to find ourselves outside the terminal building at least twice. In desperation we jumped on the inter-terminal train. When Vince spied a familiar yellow sign in the distance as we approached a station, we jumped off and gormlessly trudged towards it like weary moths determined to reach an especially alluring lightbulb.

Here we were treated to the usual insurance up-sell to cover us in the event of an alien invasion or biblical plague, given a set of keys, and pointed in the direction of the car park. This, it turned out, was about the size of England. We wandered about aimlessly like Hansel and Gretel, jabbing the unlock button on the key-fob and watching the surrounding sea of metal for signs of life.

Eventually our hire car revealed itself as a Ford of indeterminate origin – a bit like a Mondeo that had been over-inflated. We piled our luggage into the boot, reminded ourselves to call it a trunk from now on, and prepared to venture out on to the American road network.

I had little experience of driving while sat on the wrong side of a car on the wrong side of the road. And by 'little' I mean 'none.' Vince, having driven in the States before, took the first stint and expertly navigated our blue-badged barge out onto the freeway and up towards Waterbury, CT, where our Jeeps and a warm hotel were waiting for us.

As a first-time visitor to America, two things struck me as we drove the hundred miles into the heart of Connecticut. Firstly, everything looked like a film set: advertising billboards, yellow cabs, Peterbilt trucks, fire hydrants – anything I was accustomed to seeing on the silver screen looked both alien yet strangely familiar. It was as if I'd switched on the TV and accidentally fallen through the glass into an episode of *Friends*.

And the second thing? Cicadas. Watching '80s American TV shows like *Knight Rider* and *Dallas* as a kid meant I was well used to a director's staple of a night-time establishing shot with a plague of crickets chirping in the background. It was a sound I became unquestionably conditioned to associate with anything happening after dark in America. Perhaps our journey coincided with some critical moment in these deafening insects' life-cycle, but the noise was everywhere; you could even hear it on the freeway at 70mph with the windows up.

By 10pm we'd reached the workshop where our Jeeps were being prepared and met Clayton, the owner. A quick inspection of the Jeeps

All the trucks in America look like Optimus Prime.

revealed a certain amount of fettling was still needed, but this would have to wait until tomorrow.

We left the Jeeps at the workshop, bundled back into our featureless rental car and, with Clayton following, made our way to our hotel.

The Connecticut Grand Hotel's decor was dominated by an excess of gold fittings and a dazzling high-gloss sheen on every surface, but was otherwise devoid of colour or character.

I left Vince and Clayton at the bar while I endured the overly complex check-in procedure. The hotel clerk decided the best way to handle this process was to ask for each required sliver of information one piece at a time. This compelled me to make multiple trips out to the car or back into the bar to retrieve passports, driving licences, vehicle registration details, and so on. Armed with each new nugget of data I would return to reception, where the clerk would carefully make a note in the computer system.

"All done?" I enquired, hopefully.

"Almost. Now I just need your Triple-A membership card."

"I don't have one, I'm afraid."

"It says here," the clerk nodded towards her all-knowing computer screen, "that you do."

"I have an AA card, if that's any use."

She stared at me blankly as she struggled to comprehend the possibility that her computer was wrong. After an exchange of glances that indicated we'd probably both had enough of this protracted charade, she declared: "good enough."

I handed over my yellow and very British breakdown card and she dutifully shoe-horned my membership number into her computer, a process that appeared to require the addition of an extra couple of random digits to make up for the fact they were clearly different lengths.

She hit one final key on her terminal, triggering a dot-matrix printer beside her to machine-gun its way through several sheets of paper, most of which didn't seem to pertain to my booking. She tore them away from the printer with a flourish, collated them into a pile on top of which she placed two room keys as if crowning a cake with a pair of cherries, and pronounced: "have a nice stay."

I gathered the mass of accumulated documentation in my arms and retreated to the bar. There I found a cold bottle of Budweiser with my name on it, dumped the paperwork on a neighbouring stool, and took a long, lingering swig.

America, it seems, is hard work.

CHAPTER TWO

Connecticut to Philadelphia

00306⁊

YOU WOULDN'T THINK IT WOULD be possible to come up with so many different designs for the humble bathroom tap.
I know our American cousins have found it bewildering that we Brits have long since favoured having one tap for hot and another for cold, giving rise to the opportunity to simultaneously scald and freeze yourself while washing but denying the chance for a happy medium. Although many of us have now sought enlightenment through the new-fangled concept of a mixer tap, the Americans, it seems, are much more inventive.

All of which hopefully goes some way toward explaining how I'd been standing in my hotel bathroom, a toothpaste-laden toothbrush in one hand, trying to figure out how to turn the tap on.

There was only one, so it shouldn't have been that hard. Turning it didn't seem to do anything. Moving it side to side wasn't possible, and I'd already tried pushing it down. All with no joy.

On the verge of acknowledging I was a prize-winning idiot and calling reception to tell them as much, in desperation I tried lifting the tap head. Success! Boiling hot water steamed out into the basin, much of it spilling over onto the floor. Proud of my new insights into the world of foreign plumbing, I discovered twisting the head regulated the water's temperature, while pushing it down slowed the flow.

This was to become a regular game over the next few weeks. Each new motel offered their own unique take on the vagaries of water supply, and I quickly learned the seemingly limitless number of axes along which a humble tap could be moved.

I met Vince in the restaurant downstairs for breakfast. Every flat surface was covered with stainless steel trays piled high with food. Scrambled eggs, sausages, bacon – lots of bacon – something called 'grits' that looked more like porridge, and, err... cheese. Lots of cheese. If you came down to breakfast hoping to find a wide selection of cereals, fruit, yoghurt, perhaps some muesli, you'd be left wanting. But if you had a hankering for slapping pre-cut slices of bright yellow plastic cheese on top of everything, boy, were you in for a treat.

It's at this point I should probably mention pancakes. This is something I was more used to associating with a randomly-occurring Tuesday in February or March, but here it seems the entire economy is unable to function until 300 million Americans have had their pancakes. And not just one pancake – a stack. A pile. A column, even.

I never managed to find out what they were made from. It may have originally been organic at one time, but the constituent parts had long since been processed to within an inch of their lives. The main ingredient may even have its own place on the periodic table for all I know.

What I do know is that it's impossible to have pancakes by themselves. There's probably a law about this, perhaps even a line or two in the Constitution. Order pancakes in a diner and the waitress will refuse to leave until you specify a series of toppings – butter, maple syrup, toffee sauce, whipped cream, ice cream, perhaps even more pancakes. If you were feeling scandalous you could even have chopped banana,

The Wrangler looked very different to when I last saw it, but was set to be my home for the next few weeks.

strawberries, perhaps blueberries, although in the interests of ying and yang it seemed healthy options could only be supplied if they were accompanied by a liberal oozing of sweet, calorie-laden sauce.

Sensing my internal organs hadn't fully decided what time zone they were in, I opted for the less controversial choice of eggs and bacon balanced precariously on a bagel.

Checkout was thankfully a far simpler process than that of the night before, and with our bags loaded in the trunk we drove the rental car back to Clayton's workshop – a two-mile journey that involved turning the steering wheel no more than twice.

We walked round the Jeeps, making a list of the things we needed to take care of before we could hit the road and start the trip proper. Vince was in his element. As a mechanical engineer, any opportunity to grab a spanner, fiddle with the oily end of an axle, or fabricate something ingenious was not to be missed. Unfortunately that also

meant that instead of leaving on a long-planned road-trip, he and Clayton surrounded themselves with tools, welders, and bits of wiring.

Admittedly much of what made it on to our 'to do' list was quite important – fire extinguishers, for example, and CB radios so Vince and I could communicate between Jeeps.

Adam, Clayton's number two, soon impressed me. When the subject of mud-flaps came up – a legal requirement in some of the states we were driving through – he stuck a volunteering finger in the air.

"I've got this," he said, and disappeared into the back of the workshop. He came back two minutes later with a large sheet of rubber, an assortment of metal rods and brackets, a handful of nuts and bolts, some cutters, and a welder. What followed was a scene straight out of an episode of *The A-Team*.

For the uninitiated, every Saturday afternoon almost without fail saw our favourite mercenaries locked in a barn in the middle of nowhere with nothing to effect their escape other than half a tractor, a broken SodaStream machine, and a thousand cabbages. Every week, the stirring theme tune would pipe up, and an increasingly improbable montage would show the team bolting together a series of seemingly useless objects. At the end of which, the barn doors would crash open and out would fly something desperately unlikely, like an amphibious helicopter.

And so it was that, fifteen minutes later, both Jeeps had the most ingenuous bespoke mud-flaps ever devised by man. The crowning glory was that, with the removal of a quick-release pin, the flaps could be slid away from their mountings and stored inside the Jeep to stop them being ripped off on the trail.

This triumph seemed as good a time as any to stop for lunch. Vince announced that there was a subway around the corner, which puzzled me. Quite what an underground railway had to do with lunch I had no idea, but he then rattled off a long list of things at such a pace I had no idea what they were, and absolutely no hope of remembering them.

The eagle-eyed among you will notice that both Jeeps wear the same wheels and tyres for interchangeability.

It turns out that a Subway is a sandwich shop, while a sub – named after a submarine – is perhaps best described as a soft baguette about six inches long stuffed with fillings of your choice.

Luckily Tom – an editor I was working for at the time who'd come out to Clayton's to see us off – somehow caught Vince's blurted ingredient demands, and we sauntered off in the direction of Subway. Wait, who am I trying to kid? This is America we're talking about, so of course Tom and I climbed into a Cadillac with a 4.6-litre V8 engine and drove the 500 yards there.

While in Clayton's company both Jeeps had undergone substantial modifications to their suspension. The Cherokee had been shorn of its rear leaf-springs and wore more flexible coils instead, while both had grown significantly in height. Vince's Cherokee was now twelve inches further away from the ground than it was before, and he could only just see over the hood. The point of all this ground clearance and suspension flex is to allow greater axle articulation, and that helps keep the wheels (themselves now bigger than you'll find on most trucks) on the ground when tackling ambitious obstacles. Driving off-road is all about the search for grip, and if a tyre isn't on the ground, it hasn't got any traction.

As a final test we drove both Jeeps up what's known in the 4x4 world as an RTI ramp. There's some complicated maths that goes with it, but essentially the objective is to drive one wheel up a steep ramp and measure the distance that can be travelled while keeping all the other wheels on the ground. The further up the ramp the vehicle gets, the higher its Ramp Travel Index, the more capable it is off-road, and the more bragging its owner gets to do on the internet.

Frankly, it also makes for some ridiculous photos as wheels tend to end up in surprising places. But on a more practical note, it helped to assess whether minor adjustments were needed to prevent the wheels coming into contact with things they shouldn't.

This had all taken far longer than anticipated. Our overly optimistic itinerary – a print-out of which I'd been occasionally glancing at

Vince's Cherokee illustrating its new-found levels of axle articulation on the RTI ramp.

One of fourteen fuel stops we would make on our journey across America. This one was remarkably uneventful.

throughout the day in the hope that it would somehow magically change – called for us to spend only a couple of hours with Clayton before hitting the road. In the end, we'd been there almost the entire day.

However, with the testing complete and the snagging list taken care of, it was finally time for our road-trip to start. Tom took a picture for the magazine, while Adam and Clayton waved us off. It's at this point we noticed we didn't have that most basic requirement for a road-trip: fuel.

You might think getting gas would be easy. We were in America, they love the stuff. And we were driving a pair of Jeeps – what could be more American than that?

It's obvious when you think about, but when a Jeep is built to go to Europe it's tuned to run on European fuel. Back home in the UK, petrol is refined to a much higher standard than it is in the states. The closest equivalent, generally labelled 91 Premium, wasn't always available, with some gas stations only offering 85 rated fuel. To further complicate matters, in some states – like Connecticut where we were starting from – gasoline is blended with ethanol to form what's called E10, which is corrosive to our Jeeps' fuel systems. But with both the Cherokee and the Wrangler running on fumes, we had no choice but to risk it for the first of fourteen fuel stops we'd make that week.

That first visit to a gas station went without a hitch (side note: why don't British fuel pumps include a lock that clicks off automatically when the tank is full, like American ones do?). Nearly every other stop, however, would be something of a circus.

While Vince went inside to pay at our second fuel stop of the day, I sat outside in the Wrangler, patiently. On the opposite side of the gas station, I saw a guy the size of a refrigerator (not a puny British one, a great big American one – double doors, ice dispenser, the lot) suddenly clock the Jeeps as he was filling up his car. I watched with growing dread as he quickly replaced the nozzle, tightened the filler cap, and then charged across the forecourt towards me. I wasn't sure how this was going to pan out. I took the key out of the ignition in case he planned on dragging me out by my hair and making off in my freshly refuelled Jeep. As he drew closer I could see he was grinning, and by the time he was level with my door he was positively beaming. He motioned for me to wind down the window.

"Man, your Jeep is sweet!" he exclaimed, his eyes flicking over the Wrangler in an attempt to take in every detail.

"Thanks," I said with typical British reserve, trying to hide my relief at not being hauled to my death.

"I've always wanted a Jeep like this... with a winch... and a snorkel... and big tyres... and... and..." He petered out as his enthusiasm got the better of him.

"Did y'all do the work yourself?" he asked.

"Actually, we've only just picked them up. From a place in Waterbury."

He spotted my accent, tilted his head, and squinted an eye. "Where y'all from?" he quizzed.

"We're from England! We're here for a road-trip, and thought we'd bring these with us."

The mere concept of something as American as a Jeep being available in another country started to fry his mind. "You mean, y'all have Jeeps in England!?"

"Sure. They're quite popular, actually." I worried I was starting to sound like a bad Dick Van Dyke impersonator, so British did my voice sound in this unfamiliar setting.

"Wow, I thought they'd be, like, totally different, y'know."

"Well, there is this," I said, pointing to the steering wheel in front of me, on the 'wrong' side of the Jeep.

This was too much for my new gas station friend. He clasped his head in his hands, his wide eyes peering out from between his fingers as he let out a long, high-pitched "wuuuuuuut!"

Eventually he began to regain some semblance of control.

"I..." That was all he could manage at first. Shortly, this was followed by: "camera."

With that, he sprinted into the gas station and returned a few minutes later with a freshly-purchased disposable camera. He held it out by way of asking permission; it looked tiny in his huge hands. I nodded my assent and he shot every frame his miniature camera allowed in less than a minute. Spent, he returned to the driver's window and held out a shovel-like hand. I reached through the open window and shook it warmly.

"You are one crazy-ass Brit!" And with that, the human refrigerator wobbled across the forecourt and climbed back into his car.

Encounters like this soon became a regular occurrence. Every stop saw our two Jeeps put on something of a travelling sideshow that commanded a small crowd. Sometimes we didn't even need to stop to attract attention; driving along the freeway, traffic would form in clumps around us as drivers slowed to get a better look.

Jeeps are common in America. Heavily modified Jeeps are rare, although not exceptional. But two tricked-out Jeeps travelling together, both with weird-looking British license plates and no-one sitting in the driver's seat? That was unique.

We drove past a school at kicking-out time and while we negotiated our way through the school-run traffic, a group of kids noticed us. As my window was open and I was sat nearest the kerb, one of the kids called out.

"Cool Jeep, mister. Has it been turboed?"

"No, no turbo."

"Why you sittin' on the wrong side?" It was a valid question.

"We're from England," I replied.

"Where's that?"

I'd never had to explain where England is before, and it turns out it's actually quite difficult.

"It's part of the United Kingdom. You know, Great Britain."

This was met with blank stares.

"London?" I tried.

More blank stares.

"Do you know where the Queen lives? Buckingham Palace and all that?" I was clutching at straws by this point. Geography clearly wasn't a strong-point of the American education system.

"David Beckham?" I tried. This did the trick.

"Beck-ham! Beck-ham!" they all chanted, laughing. International relations restored, they ran off to find their parents.

Roads in America, I soon discovered, can be confusing. Even urban roads can be wider than the M25, and it didn't seem unusual for lanes to suddenly disappear without warning. Sometimes the right-hand lane would peel off to some unannounced destination, while other times a huge flyover would appear in the middle of the interstate, lifting the traffic away to God knows where. More than once Vince and I became separated as our two lanes diverged, only to reunite a few miles later with no obvious explanation.

Approaching a tangle of tarmac ribbons that would put Birmingham's Spaghetti Junction to shame, the satnav perched on top of the Wrangler's dashboard went into meltdown.

"Objects in mirror may be... oh, another Jeep."

"In 200 feet, take the exit. Then, take the exit. Then turn left. Then, take the exit. Take the exit!"

I looked down to see what on earth had prompted this navigational madness. The screen was a mass of lines, as if the cartographer responsible had wanted to go home early and, rather than accurately plot the road as it was, took a pen, scribbled back and forth a hundred times, and declared: 'close enough.' The satnav looked like an exploded Etch-a-Sketch, and was about as useful, too.

Vince's satnav had had the same nervous breakdown. There were no road signs. We were completely at the mercy of Lady Luck. Somehow she got us through, but it highlighted the need for us to stick together.

This wasn't made any easier by the impossibly short slip-roads. In the UK, it's expected that traffic in lane one would move over to allow cars to join the carriageway, but in America a kind of telepathically coordinated free-for-all seemed to orchestrate people's movements.

Crossing an impressive freeway bridge, a large truck caught my eye. A battered rubbish lorry of sorts, it was approaching the interstate from a slip-road to our right. And at speed. The front door was slid open, and I could see the driver hunched over the steering wheel. It was as if he was bracing himself for something.

"Have you spotted that truck to your right?" I called out to Vince over the radio, concerned they were both about to occupy the same strip of tarmac. "He looks very determined."

"Yeah, got him."

With that, the truck hit a large depression in the road, launching the front wheels skyward. As the truck landed, it sunk down on to its springs and rebounded with equal force, nearly flinging the driver out of the open door. Hanging on for dear life, he wrestled with the wheel, somehow managing to steer his bucking bronco around the tight corner of the slip-road, and joined the freeway alongside us. I glanced at him as we overtook; his expression was calm as a Hindu cow, as if this were an everyday occurrence.

Away from the interstate at a convenient set of traffic lights, I glanced at the itinerary. We were at least six hours behind schedule, and that was despite cutting our plans to the bone. We had hoped to head back into New York and eat at the Cheyenne Diner, the famous chrome and neon eatery that grew out of a railroad car. We wanted to park the Jeeps as close as we could to the Statue of Liberty for photos, but we knew getting there would be a nightmare and we'd been chasing the clock since before we even got off the plane.

We were determined, however, to make it into Philadelphia to meet up with friends Nicola and Eric. This determination nearly proved to be our undoing.

Simply getting there was hard enough. Philadelphia's road network looked like the design for a complex circuit board, the buildings standing in for electrical components like giant resistors and capacitors. The road signs did little to help – they pointed towards individual road names rather than nearby destinations, and terms like Vine Street Expressway and Benjamin Franklin Parkway meant little to us.

It was beautiful, though. The tree-lined streets were like golden archways of autumnal colour, and whatever foliage had already fallen formed a russet carpet that came alive and danced around our wheels as we drove over it. This was how I imagined Boston. At least once I wondered if we'd taken a wrong turn and ended up in the wrong city.

Parking was something of a problem, however. As we threaded the Jeeps through the maze of one-way streets looking for a space, I noticed a white van take up station behind me. I could just make out the light bar on its roof, and after it followed us through a series of right turns, I could see the livery as it flashed under a streetlight.

"The cops are behind me, I think we're going to get pulled," I called out to Vince over the radio.

I'd barely replaced the mic when my rear-view mirror filled with piercing blue light.

"Yup! Pulled!"

We took a final right turn off the narrow one-way street onto a main road and pulled over. Two cops jumped out of the van and surged towards us. Both had their hands on their holstered firearms. One made his way towards what he expected to be the Wrangler driver's door, but Vince – who'd been ahead in the Cherokee – headed him off.

"Your vehicles are in breach of Pennsylvania state vehicle code and you are driving illegally without proper vehicle tags," the cop bawled. Before Vince could respond, he added: "Your vehicles will be impounded."

We knew driving through Pennsylvania would be one of the toughest parts of our trip. The Keystone State was known for its strict vehicle code, and the Jeeps violated nearly every part of it – tyres, bumpers, lights, the fact the steering wheel was in the wrong place, the lot. Not only that, but they were still wearing their British number plates rather than proper US 'tags.'

Technically, we weren't breaking any laws. A federal exemption allowed non-residents to temporarily import a vehicle that doesn't meet local regulations for personal use, as long as it is exported again within one year. Vince made many attempts to return to his Cherokee to grab the paperwork to prove it, but the cop wasn't interested. He was dead serious. As far as he was concerned, our Jeeps weren't just about to be impounded, but crushed, too.

Sometimes in life, what seemed like a good idea at the time is often followed by the question of why more people don't already do it. Surely, there must be a reason why more people don't bring their vehicles with them when travelling to the US? As it turns out, there is. And we'd just discovered it the hard way.

The catalogue of minor calamities we'd experienced on the trip so far began to well up inside me. Sat in the Jeep, on the side of the road, with an armed cop glaring at me, it was as if the universe had tried to warn me – the delayed flight, the near-rejection at JFK, the difficulty finding fuel, the many near-misses on the freeways, the exploding satnavs. Maybe we should have paid more attention and turned back, because now the Jeeps were going to be taken from us and turned into saucepans.

The second cop, who'd so far been content to let his partner do the shouting for the both of them, shone his flashlight over the Wrangler. He checked the back seats were empty, then approached what he imagined to be the passenger door. As he trained the beam in through the window, I wound it down.

"Good evening," I offered, in my best English accent.

Surprised, he jumped back and aimed the flashlight straight into my eyes. I swear I thought I was going to be shot in the face. Gradually he lowered the beam until it hit the steering wheel in front of me.

"What in the *hell* is that doing there!?" he snorted.

"Yeah, we're from England. We're a crazy bunch, we drive on the other side of the road over there," I replied, trying to add a little levity to our situation.

He moved closer to gain a better look at the interior, and let out a long, low whistle as he tried to comprehend the mirror image before him.

"Crazy... just crazy," he breathed. "Is anything else different? Is it still a four-litre?"

A small chink of light appeared at the far end of the tunnel of our predicament – this cop must know something about Jeeps if he knew to ask about the four-litre engine.

"That's just the same. It's basically steering and lights that are different. They're still made over here, too."

He shook his head at the wonder of it all. "Must be weird changing gear with the wrong hand."

"No stranger than if I drove an American one, it's just a case of what you're used to." I sensed I was beginning to build at least some kind of rapport with this one, although it looked like Bad Cop was still hell-bent on impounding the crap out of us.

Good Cop nodded.

"So do you guys drive 'em on the beach back home?"

I was a little surprised by the question. And not just because where we used to drive them appeared spectacularly irrelevant given we were about to lose them for good.

"God no, that would be illegal."

Good Cop seemed more amazed at our killjoy laws than he did by anything else that was happening that evening. He made me explain about byways and The Crown Estate, a difficult subject to cover at the best of times. I was just relieved to see him take his hand off his gun.

"Man, you gotta go check out the Outer Banks."

The Outer Banks, he explained, were a 200-mile long series of barrier islands somewhere off the coast of North Carolina, often called America's First Beach. As well as offering water sports, hiking, and even golf, they are home to a network of routes for off-road vehicles. Judging by his growing level of excitement the more he talked about them, they must be very special indeed. I promised to check them out if we ever made it out of Philadelphia alive.

The chink of light grew a little bigger when he let slip that his partner "can get a little excited, but is basically a fair guy."

It seemed Vince was having some luck of his own, too. Bad Cop had realised his paperwork wasn't designed for confiscating British vehicles, and our combined stack of vehicle registrations, driving licences and insurance certificates were all beginning to paint a picture of a world of hassle he could probably do without. When Vince announced that we were leaving the state anyway, that sealed the deal.

"Get out of here," he demanded. We'd been reprieved, but not before he added: "Just don't expect the next cop to be so understanding." If this was an understanding cop, I'd hate to be stopped by a difficult one, I thought to myself.

We climbed back into the Jeeps, grateful that we still could, and just had time to meet up with Nicola and Eric for one quick drink in a bar before our banishment commenced.

Our itinerary called for us to be in Somerset by now, but that was 250 miles and four hours away. We were tired, and still had the cop's words ringing in our ears. Nicola kindly found us a motel in Valley Forge that was easy to get to, so we said our goodbyes and hit the road – desperate to not see another cop car.

On the way out of Philly, I became separated from Vince by a red light. The road we were travelling on seemed to criss-cross four other roads all at the same time, each with up to three lanes. At each intersection was a traffic light. Vince made it across in one go but as I approached the middle, the lights flicked instantly to red and the Cherokee's tail-lights disappeared into the distance. Bafflingly, there didn't seem to be much room for a car to stop without blocking the adjacent road. I crammed the Wrangler into the available space as best I could and waited as cars drove around me, hoping not to see anything that looked like a blue light. I have no doubt any Philadelphia local could explain what I had done wrong, but to me the road layout was completely nonsensical. Thankfully, the lights released me before I could get arrested and I caught up with Vince on the way to the freeway.

We soon found the Motel 6. Its blue and red illuminated '6' shone out like a long-anticipated lighthouse above the traffic and we pulled off the interstate towards it. We might have found our motel, but in a cruel final twist, we couldn't find the entrance. Someone seemed to have put another building in the way. We drove around the block to examine our options, but still there was no obvious way of getting in.

"Vince," I started on the radio.

"Yeahhhhh..."

"Look, we're driving two of the most capable off-road vehicles on the planet. We can't possibly be stymied by a missing piece of tarmac. All that separates us from a good night's sleep is a couple of kerbs and a grassy bank. I vote for just driving over it all."

Vince was more reluctant. If anyone complained about the tyre tracks, there'd be two very conspicuous off-roaders parked in the car park. One run-in with the cops was enough. It was a fair point. I was all for not being nearly arrested again. I backed up along the slip road just to make sure I hadn't missed anything. As I did, I spotted something in the passenger door mirror – a tiny sign that said 'enter'.

One of the challenges of driving a lifted Jeep is that anything low to the ground is essentially invisible. With the 35-inch spare tyre on the back, it's even possible for an entire car to be obscured from view. Motel 6's tiny blue sign was no doubt perfectly positioned for drivers of a left-hand-drive car, but to anyone in a right-hand-drive Jeep, to all intents and purposes it did not exist.

"Found it," I sang out over the radio.

We followed the sign through the trees and eventually the brilliant white oasis that was our motel appeared before us.

There are two facts that had a bearing on our stay here. Firstly, Nicola has a great sense of humour. And secondly, Vince snores. A lot. Luckily for the residents of Philadelphia, on this particular night the Motel 6 was almost empty, but as a joke, Nicola and the reception staff had placed Vince at one end of the building, while my room was as far away as it was physically possible to be. It was even on a different floor. We both appreciated the joke – there was certainly no way Vince's snoring was going to bother me that night.

I collapsed on to the bed, my boots still on my feet. Frankly, my room could have been next to a Bruce Springsteen concert for all I cared at this point.

CHAPTER THREE

Philadelphia to Terre Haute

010062

I HAD A FITFUL NIGHT'S sleep. For some reason I kept having dreams about being in prison. I remember clinging to the bars of my cell, only to be told by the warden – who bore an uncanny resemblance to the warden in *Shawshank Redemption* – that they'd been made from a melted-down Jeep. Morgan Freeman was in the next cell, and after lights out he told me to 'get busy driving, or get busy dying.' Thankfully at this point I woke up.

The Motel 6 didn't disappoint with its unfathomable taps, this time for the shower, until I discovered that the temperature lever that sprouted from the wall could be pulled as well as turned.

Vince had already checked out for the both of us, and I found him in the car park packing up the Cherokee. We had a lot of miles to cover to make up for yesterday and we were keen to make a start. We skipped the motel breakfast and picked up the I-76 westward, making good on our promise to last night's cops to 'get the hell out of here.'

Vince preferred to lead so I assumed the role of tail-end Charlie in our attention-grabbing two-Jeep convoy. Once we'd notched up a hundred miles or so between us and the Philly cops, Vince pulled us off the interstate and headed for a small town. I say 'town' but as a simple country boy everything still seemed colossal to me. The main road was three lanes wide, there were truck dealerships with hundreds of new pick-ups on the sprawling forecourt, and a Walmart the size of Berkshire. Eateries of every conceivable kind were sprinkled at hundred yard intervals – doughnut shops, waffle houses, spice bars (no, I don't know what they are either) – while every venue boasted its own vast car park. Every other venue was a drive-through; a drive-through coffee bar, complete with elevated windows for serving trucks, a drive-through truck-wash in a building that looked like it once housed the space shuttle, even a drive-through bank. There were absolutely no sidewalks, though.

While I was trying to take all of this in, Vince had clearly been looking for something. We'd already performed a couple of slightly questionable U-turns and upset at least one trucker in the process.

"Are we looking for something in particular, Vince?" I asked over the radio.

"It's here somewhere!"

"What is?" I demanded, after the third U-turn.

"Got it!" he exclaimed.

I wasn't sure what we'd found as we pulled into another giant parking lot. At the entrance, a towering yellow and red sign pierced the grey, featureless sky. 'Denny's,' it announced. The name wasn't familiar to me. I didn't realise it at the time, but Denny's would soon become a great friend of ours.

Denny's is a diner. In fact, their tag-line declares themselves to be 'America's diner.' Vince had clearly been looking forward to this, and after Sheila greeted us at the door, seated us in a booth and handed us a pair of giant menus, I could start to see why. Everything had a name that championed its gut-busting qualities – The Grand Slam Slugger, The Grand Slamwich, and so on. Just as well, because I was so hungry

I felt sure I could eat a horse. If I'd looked hard enough there was probably one on the menu, but instead I settled for something billed as the Wild West Omelette. Sheila, though, was insistent I had pancakes to go with it. We were in America; it would have been illegal not to.

Our breakfast could easily have been dismissed as not just a heart-attack on a plate, but probably also an embolism of some kind with a side-order of angina. But it tasted good, didn't cost the earth, and came with a smile at every Denny's we stopped at. On days when we were still on the road 16 hours later and everywhere else had shut, that counted for a lot, I can tell you.

With full bellies, we flopped back into the Jeeps and wobbled back to the interstate. Unfortunately, we didn't get very far.

From my now usual position behind Vince's Cherokee, I spied the occasional wisp of smoke coming from somewhere underneath.

"I could be wrong," I said to Vince over the radio, "but there might be smoke coming from your Jeep."

There was silence for a few seconds. The Cherokee kept on driving.

"Is it a lot?" Vince replied, finally.

"Seems to be the occasional whiff, rather than huge billowing clouds."

"Smoke or steam, would you say?"

"I'd say smoke. It's hard to see, but it might be blue, so I guess it's oil."

"Oil pressure looks fine. We'd better check."

We found a service area and pulled into the parking lot next to a stock Wrangler that was soon dwarfed by our modified Jeeps.

There's only so much crawling around on the ground in a service area can tell you. Although we could see a small amount of oil on the exhaust which was quickly burnt off leading to the tell-tale blue smoke, the source wasn't immediately apparent. The engine oil level looked good, none of the gaskets were weeping, it had all the hallmarks of a mystery. We decided to carry on but would keep a close eye on it.

Vince, who can only just see over the bonnet of his Cherokee, investigates the oil leak.

Since we'd stopped, we pulled into the gas station to fill up while we were there. Despite the huge tyres and the aerodynamics of a Portacabin, both Jeeps were averaging around 240 miles to a tank.

As usual, our presence in the gas station didn't go unnoticed. The driver of a late '80s Cherokee sauntered over to inspect Vince's Jeep, and he spent the next twenty minutes admiring it in minute detail. He peered inside the wheel-arches, checked out the snorkel, under the front bumper, behind the rear tyre carrier. Everything. Vince was inside where he'd drawn a crowd of his own as he recounted the story of our journey. His audience whooped in disbelief when he explained that we're used to paying the equivalent of $9 for a gallon of gas back home – in the US, we were paying roughly $2.50.

Vince's Cherokee had also drawn the affections of a very young-looking driver in a red pick-up. He looked no more than fifteen years old and was dwarfed by his huge truck. I found myself wondering if he needed wooden blocks on his shoes to reach the pedals, like Short Round in *Indiana Jones*. He seemed keen to show off to us and screeched out of the gas station at full throttle, leaving behind a giant number eleven on the tarmac and a thick cloud of black smoke that had belched from his exhaust. It hung in the air for some time after the pickup had long disappeared out of sight; long enough for us to have to drive through it as we made our own, rather more restrained exit.

This level of interest continued back on the interstate, too. A white truck pulled alongside us, presumably to admire the Jeeps. It tracked us from the adjacent lane for some minutes, its driver apparently oblivious to the queue that was forming behind him. In England, horns would have been sounded and gesticulating fingers flicked out of windows, but here, no-one seemed to mind.

Eventually the truck drew alongside Vince, ahead of me in the Cherokee. I watched as the passenger window was wound down and a face appeared. Then an arm. As the truck finally started pulling away, the passenger began waving enthusiastically. So enthusiastically, in fact, that to maintain his view he had to lean further and further out of the window. Still waving, he lost his grip on the door and nearly fell out of the cab. All we could do was wave back and pray he didn't drop to the tarmac to be run over by his own truck.

One freeway encounter had us baffled for days. But first, an observation on American brand loyalty.

In America, pickup trucks are everywhere. It's not hard to see why: this is a big country, and there's work to be done, so Americans quite rightly want a vehicle they can depend on. We Brits might be content with an estate car for the occasional trip to the tip on a Sunday morning, but in the US a pickup is a vehicle with a job to do. Often that job is bigger than you might imagine, and it's not unusual to see them

We left the Jeeps to cool down while we went inside and flooded Burger King.

kitted out with a 'fifth wheel' – a horseshoe-shaped trailer coupling Brits are more used to seeing on the back of an articulated lorry – together with an extra set of wheels on the rear axle, making a wide-body pickup called a 'dually.'

Much like a rancher might have a favourite stallion, so too do Americans have a favourite pickup. And it's tribal. If your family always bought Chevrolets, you would too, whereas if your daddy had a Ford, you'd forever be a Ford man. In fact, Ford sold nearly a million F-Series pickups last year, so the numbers involved are huge.

That tribal loyalty spills out on to other brands, too. Some might have unwavering faith in their Ford Bronco, while others would only ever drive a Jeep. What we discovered that Tuesday afternoon was that, apparently, in the US there exists something of a 'them' and 'us' between Cherokee and Wrangler owners.

I could hear the huge dually pickup approaching from about a mile away. Smoke was erupting from its exhaust like a Union Pacific Big

Boy – 'rolling coal,' they call it, I found out later. As it drew alongside the Wrangler, the driver let off the gas pedal and I could hear its huge turbos whistling as they spooled down. After a few seconds, the passenger wound down the window and, with a broad grin on his face, gave me and the Wrangler an excitable thumbs up. I waved back an acknowledgement, at which the pickup roared off towards Vince's Jeep. As the two drew level, the pickup surveyed the Cherokee for a few seconds before things took a curious turn. Rather than the thumbs up I'd been treated to, the passenger gave Vince the full Gareth Hunt coffee bean 'jerk off' hand gesture, before thundering off into the distance leaving behind nothing but the smell of unburnt diesel and two very confused Jeep drivers.

With the trail of blue smoke from Vince's Jeep becoming more obvious, we thought this might be an appropriate time to stop at a rest area for lunch, and to allow the Cherokee to cool down so we could investigate more closely.

Burger King was the sole culinary choice at this particular service area, and it was here that we discovered a sort of part self-service set-up that we'd not encountered before. Food was ordered at the counter as you'd expect, but having ordered a Coke with our burgers we were handed an empty plastic cup each and pointed in the direction of the drinks machines. These were arranged along the wall across from the counter in what we assumed was a kind of 'all you can drink' free refill arrangement.

Vince placed his cup under the appropriate nozzle and pushed it against the dispenser's lever, prompting Coke to flow out of the machine and into his cup. So far so good. When Vince felt his standard-issue bucket contained the requisite level of calorie overload, he pulled it away from the machine, releasing the lever. Except the machine disagreed with him, and it continued to gush cola like a caffeine-flavoured fountain of incontinence.

Vince has a very logical mind and as a mechanical engineer he was keen to establish what he was doing wrong. To help him achieve this, he summoned me to leave my now half-eaten burger and accompany

Axle oil forced out of the breather tube by the high temperatures was dripping onto the exhaust.

him to the drinks machine. Taking my as yet unfilled cup, he proceeded to demonstrate his syrupy predicament – just as before, the machine continued to spew chilled soda until long after the cup was removed, and no amount of wrestling with it could convince it to stop. Fearing we might flood all of Pennsylvania with sticky, carbonated water, we decided it would be best if we ate the rest of our lunch outside.

After lunch, the Cherokee had cooled down sufficiently so we could crawl underneath it without attracting third-degree burns. This revealed that the substance burning on the exhaust was in fact axle oil.

Non-technical readers should look away now, because here comes the science bit. For Vince's Cherokee to safely accommodate its larger tyres without snapping its axles like cotton buds, they'd been upgraded somewhat. The rear axle was now a Ford 8.8, first developed (by Ford, strangely enough) back in the 1980s for heavy-duty applications like high-powered Mustangs and pickups, and had remained in use until only very recently. It's a popular swap for all kinds of modified vehicles, not just Jeeps, because it's strong as hell, parts for it are cheap and, having been in production for decades, is relatively easy to get hold of. In common with most axles, it includes a vent or breather that allows air to enter and leave the axle housing as it expands and contracts with heat. But to prevent mud and muck being sucked into the axle, a length of flexible pipe is attached to this breather with the open end fixed somewhere higher up out of harm's way. On Vince's Cherokee, this breather line terminated at the back of the engine bay against the bulkhead. The smoke, we discovered, was caused by the oil expanding in the axle sufficiently to force it up and out of the breather line where it would run down the bulkhead and drip onto the hot exhaust. The permanent fix would involve adding an oil catcher for the breather line, but for now we could safely ignore the wisps of blue smoke until the axle had found its new oil level. With the mystery solved, we left the flooded Burger King behind and returned to the safety of the interstate.

Oil leaks aside, both Jeeps were remarkably well behaved, despite being well outside their comfort zone for hundreds of miles at a time on the freeways. Their 35-inch mud terrain tyres were hardly well suited to hour after hour of concrete, but it was something Vince and I were by now well used to. The Wrangler's shorter wheelbase did lend it a certain *laissez-faire* attitude to road holding and lane discipline. The Cherokee, I imagined, was probably comfort personified. They did both struggle with the steeper sections of the I-76, however.

"I'd love to know what engine they put in these trucks," said Vince over the radio as one blasted past us.

The Kenilworths and Peterbilts seemed to glide up even the steepest climbs, usually without the slightest deviation from their 70mph cruise. The Wrangler, however, would easily get bogged down in third gear during a prolonged ascent, while the Cherokee's automatic transmission would constantly hunt up and down in a desperate search for a ratio that would help it reach the summit.

By the time we crossed in to Indiana – our fourth state of the day – we were beginning to struggle, too. It was nearly 10pm, but with 150 miles still to go to our overnight stop in Terre Haute, all we could do was pull into a rest area for a celebratory can of Red Bull, before heading back out on to I-70.

At least the Hoosier state rewarded us with a smoother road surface than Ohio. For much of the last 250 miles, the seams in the concrete had announced their presence in the Jeep's cabin like a metronomic drum beat. As the day wore on the heartbeat of the highway had become almost soporific, but it was a relief when, precisely on the state line, the drumming ceased as cement gave way to lush, black asphalt. At least for a while, anyway.

Indianapolis passed by in a blur of interchanges and off-ramps. We pulled into a truck stop just beyond the city to refuel and discovered more than just a mere gas station – we'd arrived at a 'travel plaza.' About the size of a large village, the site included several restaurants, a truck service centre, a tyre shop, an RV waste dump, and a retail presence that would put many an airport to shame. We wandered around it for a while, marvelling at the sheer array of goods on offer: cowboy boots, power tools, microwaves, hunting rifles, CD players, oil filters, truck nutz (look that one up at your peril) and a range of alcohol that would have many a British copper reaching for their breathalyser.

With the end in sight, we pushed on towards Terre Haute and arrived at our Super 8 motel just after midnight.

We'd driven over 700 miles that day.

CHAPTER FOUR

Terre Haute to Abilene

`01564`2

I KNOCKED ON THE DOOR to Vince's room and he opened it in a mild state of frustration. He'd been trying to connect his laptop to the motel Wi-Fi so he could check the details of our route, but hadn't been having much luck.

"Do me a favour," he asked, "ring down to reception and ask them what the Wi-Fi password is. I've asked them already but it doesn't seem to work."

I merrily picked up the handset and dialled reception. It rang for a while, and was eventually answered with a deep sigh.

"Yes?" the receptionist barked, impatiently.

"Oh, hi there. I wonder if you could tell me what the Wi-Fi password is please?"

There was another sigh, this time filled with irritation and followed by a long pause.

"Hello? Are you still..." I was interrupted.

43

Our trip covered so many miles we had to get the Jeeps serviced part way through.

"As I've already told you... it's Johnboy... capital J, and a zero for the first o."

Before I could respond with a "thank-you" the handset was slammed down at the other end.

Now a little deaf in one ear, I hung up and turned to Vince. "It's Johnboy, capital J, and a zero for the first o."

"That's what I thought they said, but it doesn't seem to work."

"How many times have you asked them?" I enquired.

Vince made himself look busy as he fiddled with the network settings on his laptop.

"A few," he admitted.

Recognising that the problem probably resided with his laptop and not in the precise pronunciation of Johnboy, Vince packed away his things and we left the room. As we walked through reception and returned our room keys, the staff glared at us furiously.

"There go those idiots who can't even understand their own language," I imagined them to be saying to each other. We didn't have time to hang around to find out, because we had somewhere to be.

We were doing so many miles on this trip that both Jeeps were now due a service. For once we'd planned ahead and made a booking at the Burger Chrysler dealership to have both Jeeps' essential fluids changed.

British dealers could learn a thing or two from these guys. For a start, all the staff were fascinated both by our Jeeps and the story of our trip. An older gentleman we assumed to be the service manager asked many questions about where we'd been and where we were going next, and then presented us with key rings as souvenirs.

Vince's Cherokee had developed a fault with one of the tail-lights and the technician volunteered to take a look as part of the service. We watched as he pulled out the factory service manual and methodically ran through the diagnostic procedure, eventually narrowing the fault down to a damaged wiring harness that he expertly repaired. Without prompting he also wired up the new license plate light that we ran out of time to attend to two days ago.

Preferring to get out of everyone's hair and leave them to it, we retired to the customer lounge. There we met a lady waiting for her Liberty to be serviced. After recounting our story again – something we'd managed to get down to a couple of compact sentences thanks to all the practice – we asked if she could recommend anywhere for breakfast.

"There's an IHOP just around the corner," she said.

Of course, this meant nothing to us, but the way she pronounced it 'eye-hop' conjured images of some Apple-branded pogo-stick convention.

"Yeah, I think it stands for International House of Pancakes."

This, I have to admit, sounded incredible. More incredible even than an iPogo. Because this wasn't just a pancake shop, it was an *international* pancake shop.

"Awesome! Is it close enough for us to walk there?" we asked her.

"Sod this weekend!" After the hundreds of miles we'd driven to get here, we agreed with this sentiment.

She looked at us blankly. Walking clearly wasn't the done thing around here.

"Well, you could, I suppose. It's not far."

Less than a third of a mile, in fact, but as we discovered there were no pavements. We took our lives into our hands crossing the four-lane highway outside the Jeep dealership, probably committing the offence of 'jaywalking' in the process, and trudged along the grass verge.

After less than a hundred yards, Vince broke down into an uncontrollable fit of laughter. Unable to speak, barely able to breathe, when I asked him what he was laughing at he could only point. He pointed to a roadside sign belonging to a garden centre – The Blooms Brothers – its movie theatre-style lettering advertising an upcoming promotion.

"Sod this weekend," it said. Clearly this meant something very different in America, but is certainly not a phrase any British garden centre would get away with.

The IHOP was clearly a popular spot for breakfast in Terre Haute. The parking lot was full, but our waitress managed to find us a table from which she hurriedly cleared away the previous customers' leftovers.

It turns out the IHOP caters for more than just pancake fanciers. Waffles, crepes, melts, omelettes, the biggest burgers I've ever seen in my life, even salads. But we were in America, in an institution called the International House of Pancakes. We'd probably have been deported if we ordered anything else.

A customer on the next table ordered something called 'the full stack.' What arrived a few minutes later was a pile of pancakes almost a foot high, dripping from top to bottom in syrup, crowned by a dollop of whipped cream. I could feel my arteries clogging up just at the sight of it. By contrast, we behaved ourselves and ordered something more restrained.

Our waitress returned with our pancakes and a tray laden with mysterious unlabelled black jugs and lidded containers, which she placed one by one on the table before us. Inadvertently, she had created the breakfast equivalent of the cups-and-balls magic trick, and I tentatively lifted the lid on each one to try and ascertain their contents.

Fearing there might be some unwritten pancake etiquette, I tried to surreptitiously observe the full stack customer on the next table. I watched as he unscrewed the top of one of the jugs and upended it over his pancakes. As it turned out, this choice made him rather a poor

While servicing both Jeeps, Burger Chrysler fixed a number of issues for us, including two recalls the British dealers had missed.

role model; instead of lashings of maple syrup, his pancakes were now liberally soaked with coffee. IHOP's menu includes many toppings – bananas, strawberries, blueberries, chocolate mousse, even New York cheesecake – but not coffee. His misfortune amused his companions no end but, judging by the rate at which he ate his now coffee-infused pancakes, didn't appear to detract from their flavour.

Breakfast taken care of, we sauntered back to the Jeep dealership. They'd been busy in our absence. Without being asked, they'd looked up the UK service histories of both Jeeps and discovered there were two outstanding recalls for the Wrangler – one regarding an exhaust heat-shield and the other for the ignition barrel. They'd taken care of both, free of charge, despite having to send someone to another dealership to collect a required part that wasn't in stock. They'd even fixed little stickers to the windscreens to remind us when the next services were due, although we'd likely be on the other side of the Atlantic by then.

We paid the bill gladly, during which the cashier asked us where we were off to next.

"We've got 650 miles to do now to get to Kansas," we replied.

"Would you mind waiting for just a minute more?" she asked us.

"Sure, no problem."

She soon returned with our keys and said "we're ready for you now."

We stepped outside to discover she'd assembled what appeared to be the entire staff to see us off. It was a little overwhelming. The service we'd received had been nothing short of incredible, without a doubt the best service I've ever experienced at a car dealership. They'd gone the extra mile (or ten) to help us, and the enthusiasm they shared for our journey was more than a little humbling.

We fired up the Jeeps and headed for the main road, our mirrors filled with smiling and waving. After a quick stop for gas, we pulled back on to the familiarity of the I-70.

The sheer size of the American interstate network can be difficult for us mere Brits to comprehend. The I-70 we relied on for so much of our trip, for example, is 2,151 miles long, running from Baltimore in the east to Utah in the mid-west. By comparison, the longest motorway we have in the UK is the M6, its rather piffling 232 miles running from the Midlands to just short of the Scottish border. On this trip that's the kind of distance we try to achieve before breakfast; it's merely an aperitif in road-trip terms. But then the US is a truly vast country – the 700 miles we travelled yesterday, for instance, would be enough to take us from my home town in Hampshire all the way to John o' Groats, Scotland's most northerly point. Keep driving and you'd fall in the sea.

Twenty minutes after leaving Burger Chrysler we entered Illinois, our ninth state, where we also crossed into a new time zone. We were part way through our first 25-hour day.

Precisely at the state line Indiana's smooth tarmac was cruelly snatched from us, replaced instead by drone-inducing concrete. Other than that, Illinois announced itself only with a small sign declaring it

'The Land of Lincoln' which I assumed at the time to mean America's most famous president had been born there. As it turns out, he wasn't. He was born in Kentucky, only moving to Illinois when he was 21 – ironically, from neighbouring Indiana, with which one assumes the tourist board enjoys a healthy degree of competition. More accurate might have been to declare Illinois 'The Realm of Reagan,' since he is the only president to have been born in the state.

Whatever the state's presidential preferences, it wasn't long before we were polluting it with a light misting of oil from Vince's Jeep. Of course, the rear axle had been refilled with fresh oil as part of the service that morning, and that meant it was back to forcing some of it up and out of the breather line from where it could burn on the hot exhaust.

If you're not familiar with the concept of MacGyver, he was the titular character in a 1980s TV series who had an uncanny knack of fixing things, often with the most improbable of components. He never went anywhere without a Swiss Army knife and a roll of duct-tape which, when combined with whatever was at hand, was enough to construct almost any device imaginable. Vince, it seems, has seen more than his fair share of episodes. We pulled off the interstate and into a small town where we found an auto parts store.

"I'll just be a minute," Vince said as he disappeared inside.

He returned a minute later with a short length of rubber tubing, a clamp and a few sundries. He rummaged around in the back of his Jeep for a while and produced a small bottle of water, the remnants from which he emptied out on to the road. Opening the bonnet of his Cherokee, he fixed the bottle in a convenient spot towards the back of the engine bay, extended the axle breather line using the rubber tube, and fed the open end into the bottle. Voila – an oil catcher. MacGyver would have been proud.

We knew that leaving Terre Haute late in the day would inevitably place us somewhere busy at rush hour, but there was little we could do about it. As the commuter traffic started to build, we found ourselves driving into St. Louis on the I-70, apparently at the same time as everyone else.

We should have taken the I-270 which follows a less fraught and more northerly route around the city. Instead, we found ourselves following the remnants of the I-70 right through the city centre.

The Illinois/Missouri state line follows the path of the Mississippi River. As we crossed over the river on what was admittedly a rather impressive bridge, a blue sign proudly declared "Missouri welcomes you!" I, however, had rather different sentiments in mind.

"Hey look – Misery welcomes you," I called out to Vince over the radio.

Not wishing to be rude about Missouri or its inhabitants, which I'm sure are all fine people, but my experience on the St. Louis freeways that rush hour was rather less welcoming.

"Never before have I had so many people driving at me from so many different directions, all at the same time," I complained to Vince.

The St. Louis road network seemed to consist of endless slip-roads and off-ramps, often appearing without warning and without logic.

Vince MacGyvered together a temporary solution for the recurring axle oil leak using an empty bottle and some tubing.

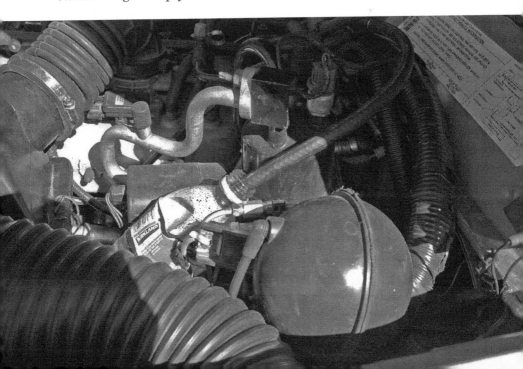

Exits weren't signed until the last minute, and if you were unlucky enough to be in the far right lane at the time, there was little chance of barging your way in to an adjacent lane. Perhaps because of this, Missourians seemed to have developed the tactic of simply driving at whoever was in the lane they liked the look of and hoping for the best. I'd had to take evasive action several times to avoid being skewered by a fast-moving and very determined SUV emerging from a side road, and it soon began to grate. Back home in the UK switching lanes to let someone in is relatively painless – flick on an indicator and the chances are someone will drop back to accommodate you. Here in Misery, the opposite appeared to be true; signalling your intention to move over saw the gap immediately disappear as everyone closed ranks around you.

After suffering from this several times, I started to deploy a new tactic: each time an errant Missourian looked at the patch of tarmac I was currently occupying with envious eyes, or so much as looked in my direction, I leant on the horn and flicked on all the auxiliary lights, illuminating the Wrangler like the loudest and most obnoxious Christmas tree ever to travel on an interstate. This seemed to do the trick, as the visibly shocked reaction of more than one driver proved. So, if you were on the I-70 that day and a Wrangler seared your retinas and blew out your eardrums, I have two things to say: firstly, I'm sorry. And secondly: tough.

Maybe there was an approved etiquette for dealing with this situation, but fending off a thousand people trying to involve us in their accidents was quite tiring. We pulled off the interstate and found a small burger outlet to hide in for a while.

Walking up to the counter to order our food, I was surprised when the teenager behind it addressed me as 'sir.' Back home these kinds of places aren't known for their service, and are usually staffed by disinterested youngsters who feel forced into a dead-end job before they can move on to something better. But this guy was smiling and enthusiastic. With our order complete, he said: "Please take a seat, I'll bring your food over as soon as it's ready."

We sat down in the otherwise empty restaurant. One minute later the teenager was back.

"Here's your food, gentlemen. Is there anything else I can get you?" he asked, as he distributed the contents of his tray between us.

"No, this all looks great, thank you very much," we replied.

"You're very welcome, please enjoy your meal." With that, the teenager left us. The contrast between the psychotic Missouri drivers and our host was dramatic. I almost felt guilty for calling the place 'Misery' and I vowed to have a more positive outlook when we returned to the I-70.

As we drew closer to Kansas City on the border between Missouri and, well... Kansas, a new trend started to develop: roadside advertising. Huge signs, bigger than a double-decker bus and elevated fifty feet or more into the air lined the interstate. On some stretches the billboards competed with each other for space, but it was the subject of the adverts that I found a little strange. One poster would declare "Jesus is alive! Call us for proof!" while the next would promote "Adult videos, next exit – truckers welcome." Guns, loans, strippers and Jesus seemed the most advertised content, but the juxtaposition of these subjects made me question who exactly I was sharing the freeway with.

As darkness fell, the simple act of staying on the freeway became a little harder. Some stretches of the interstate had been recently resurfaced using the blackest asphalt ever devised by man. Like an astrological black hole, it seemed to swallow all available light from its surroundings, and even direct illumination from our headlights failed to elevate its sheer darkness. The fact it was also freshly laid and therefore perfectly smooth only added to the eeriness. If it wasn't for the wind tugging at the canvas of the Wrangler's soft-top, it would have been much like how I imagine it feels to travel through the silence of space.

The lack of painted road markings made it difficult to judge where the lanes were, while the Wrangler's short wheelbase and already fairly pronounced waywardness made it wander across the blacktop like a wino checking dumpsters for scraps.

Sweating from the concentration required to keep our convoy pointing in roughly the right direction, we pulled into a rest area. It was midnight, and Vince suggested we allowed ourselves twenty minutes' kip before continuing.

Vince is one of those lucky people who can sleep on demand just about anywhere. I, on the other hand, need something akin to total blackout and a lack of noise, two things unlikely to be found in an interstate rest area. I tried to force myself to rest but my brain was too alert. I admitted defeat, jumped out of the Jeep and wandered over to the toilet block.

Back home in England, public toilets are likely to be of simple (and cheap) breeze-block construction with a complete absence of style or design. They're also likely to be stinky as hell and probably permanently vandalised for good measure. But here, on the side of the I-70, a hundred miles from anywhere, was a rest room that looked like it had just crash-landed from outer space. It was partially built into the hillside, while the stone-fronted façade was curved like a UFO. There was more than a touch of art deco about it, which conspired with the yellow sodium lighting to create the illusion of having stepped onto a science fiction B-movie set. Yet there was also something strangely welcoming about it. While I made use of the facilities inside, I heard a truck pull up outside. The trucker walked in as I washed my hands.

"Good evening," he said, as he walked past me and up to a urinal.

Starting a conversation in a men's room is fairly near the top of the list of things not to do, according to the unpublished book of 'Stuff to Know as a Man.' But what the hell, this wasn't a men's room, it was a spaceship.

"Hello," I replied, cagily. There was silence for a while as he attended to his business and I splashed water on my face in an attempt to remove some of the accumulated stress of the last few hours.

"That wouldn't happen to be your Jeep outside, would it?" he asked, over his shoulder.

I dabbed at my face with a paper towel. "The Wrangler, yes it is," came my muffled response.

"That's a nice ride. Where yer headed?" he asked, zipping up his fly and approaching the row of sinks. He observed the other unwritten rule about not using a sink or urinal next to another man if one further away was available. Our conversation, therefore, continued through the safety of the mirror before us.

"Utah eventually, but we're hoping to get to Abilene tonight," I said, drying my hands in readiness for a quick exit.

He pulled a paper towel out of the dispenser, but before he used it he turned to face me square on. "Y'all need to be careful out there. There's a storm coming in. Looks like a big one, too."

As men's room encounters go, this one was turning out to be strangely useful. He continued: "I'm gonna park up here for the night, trucks and storms don't mix well."

I thanked him for the warning and wished him a good night.

"Take care," he said as I left the rest room.

Vince was fast asleep in the Cherokee. It had been more than twenty minutes since we stopped, and I tapped gently on the window to get his attention. He woke with a start that looked more like a heart-attack.

"We'd better get a move on," I said, "apparently there's a storm coming."

The trucker wasn't wrong.

Much of the I-70 from this point was arrow-straight. Occasionally it rose along a subtle gradient and from the crest we could see for miles in every direction. The skies were pitch black; not a single star pierced the night, while even the road ahead of us was untroubled by tail-lights. We could see cars and trucks pulling off the road into service areas, huddling together like ladybirds preparing to clamp down their shells and ride out the winter in hibernation. I had the overwhelming feeling that they knew something we didn't.

At that moment, the reason became clear. Far off in the distance, some miles away where the I-70 met the horizon, was a biblical lightning storm. Huge strands of intense orange forked down to the ground, one after the other as if part of a relentless attack, each one revealing silhouettes of otherwise hidden buildings and water towers as their glow spread out towards us.

"I bet that's where our motel is," I said to Vince over the radio, half-joking. Neither of us had ever seen orange lightning before. And it was the only thing on this road besides us.

The storm was pushing the Wrangler across the road like a kitten swiping at a ball of wool, and occasionally something whipped up by the wind would clatter against the side of the Jeep.

We pulled off the interstate to reduce the impact of the sidewinds, but the reality was whichever road we chose, we were the only ones on it. We had become an unwitting pair of storm-chasers.

I rounded a corner just as a powerful gust blew a thick cloud of dust across the road, consuming the Jeep and utterly obliterating my vision. I couldn't see the road, I couldn't tell what direction the Jeep was pointing in, I had no alternative but to stop where I was and hope nothing (like a falling tree or an airborne house) hit me.

Vince saw the Wrangler's headlights disappear from his rear-view mirror.

"Christ, where are you?" his voice over the radio the only thing that penetrated the dust cloud.

"I'm in my own personal storm," I replied, trying to sound calm, "I'll be right with you."

Newspaper headlines flashed before my eyes: "British duo die after driving Jeeps into tornado." "English idiots lost after trying to outrun twister."

We should have stopped. We should have turned back. But when it's 3am and you've been driving for nearly 600 miles, you become detached from reality, like everything's just a video game.

Glad to still be alive and on the ground, we pulled into Abilene and found our motel. Behind it, the sign for a bowling hall caught my eye.

"Tornado Alley."

CHAPTER FIVE

Abilene to
Florence

02048?

"**B**OLLOCKS TO THE ITINERARY," I said to myself, "I'm having a lie-in."

The miles were beginning to take their toll, and after 700 of them yesterday, I felt I'd earned a little extra time in bed. Vince must have had similar thoughts, because he didn't emerge from his room until later in the morning, either.

Luckily, the itinerary didn't have too much of a problem with our decision. It called for a 'mere' 480 miles that day, but by the sounds of the wind and rain that lashed against my motel room window, much of it was set to take place against the backdrop of a tornado warning still very much in effect.

Opposite our motel was a large gas station and a 24/7 'travel store.' We topped off the Jeeps and sauntered casually around its aisles, part of our determination to have a more relaxed start to the day. The Wrangler's steering wheel was still covered in oil from its time in Clayton's workshop, and I'd spent much of the last 1,500 miles kicking myself for not cleaning it off before leaving. I bought some wet-wipes so I could finally cross that one off my list, and then went into battle with the world's most complicated coffee machine.

It seemed to exist on multiple levels with elevated platforms, dispensers at various heights, and a series of disjointed surfaces festooned with buttons that did little to give away their purpose. I tentatively placed an empty cup under what looked like a dispensing nozzle and pressed a button marked with what I hoped was a coffee bean symbol. Nothing happened. I tried another nozzle and this time pressed a button that wore a hand-written 'Hot Chocolate' label. Again, nothing happened. I began to wonder if this was the beverage equivalent of the fairground game of whack-a-mole where furry critters appear at random in surprising locations, requiring the reactions of a trained ninja to catch them. Having tried two more buttons but still been ignored by this vast non-dispensing machine, I went to consign my cup to the bin. It was at this point I noticed a powdery residue at the bottom. This fearsomely complicated machine, bristling with every conceivable flavour, had been depositing small helpings of instant coffee and other powders into my cup with each button press. But nowhere that I could see was there the facility to add that one most basic ingredient – water. Fearing I might be charged four times for what would presumably now be the most disgusting cup of coffee ever served, I surreptitiously abandoned my cup and left with my wet-wipes.

It was still raining heavily with gale-force winds as we left Abilene for our old friend the I-70. We pulled onto the interstate and I shifted the Wrangler into fifth gear. As I did so, I heard a sound I wasn't expecting – a splash – that had definitely come from inside the Jeep. I looked down and could see water sloshing around my feet. I was effectively piloting a four-wheel-drive puddle down the freeway.

"Vince, would you mind if we stopped for a sec?" I asked over the radio. "There's a lot of water in here."

The tornado warning was still in effect as we left Abilene the next morning under stormy skies heavy with rain.

We'd only gone ten miles, and here we were, already pulling into a rest area. I opened the door and tipped out the contents of the floor tray.

"Wow, did you leave a window open in the middle of a tornado?" A not unreasonable question for Vince to ask, given we'd parked up at 3am and were probably too tired to care.

"Everything was definitely shut, and the top's done up properly. The seat's dry, too, so it's not come in through the windows."

Wranglers aren't known for being entirely weather-tight, but this was a lot of water to have inside any car. I felt all around the carpets in case it was coming in from underneath. At floor level everything was dry, but the carpet against the bulkhead was sopping. Such was the

Ominous skies, left over from yesterday's tornado, accompanied us for much of our journey through Kansas.

ferocity of the wind and rain overnight that it had, we supposed, forced its way in through the base of the windscreen from where it could run down behind the dashboard and collect on the floor. But there was little we could do about it parked in a rest area.

"Let's just keep going, we can look at it properly somewhere less... hurricaney. Everything appears to be working OK," I suggested.

Famous last words. Because not everything was working OK. We returned to the I-70 and, as we accelerated back up to speed, I pressed the button on the steering wheel to engage cruise control and took my foot off the gas.

The Jeep slowed down.

Assuming I'd not pressed it properly, I tried again. The Jeep still slowed down.

"Vince," I called out cagily over the radio. "You know I said everything was working OK?"

There was a pause. "Yeahhhhh..?"

"The cruise control doesn't."

The water may have shorted it out, but either way I was forced to drive the next thousand miles with my foot on the gas pedal. Hardly life-threatening, I grant you, but certainly uncomfortable.

Although officially known as the sunflower state, Kansas is really the wheat state. Nearly a fifth of America's wheat crop is grown here which, once harvested, is stored in huge silos that litter the countryside like an army of patient missiles, standing ready to participate in a war that never comes. Locally they're known by the rather more romantic title 'prairie cathedrals' which perhaps also hints at the slightly religious esteem with which the occupation of farming is held in these parts.

The scale of farming operations here is truly mind-boggling. The average farm is nearly 750 acres in size with the industry contributing more than $18 billion to the local economy. The equipment needed to produce this is also massive: huge centre-pivot irrigation booms stretch out for more than quarter of a mile as they slowly rotate around their crops, while giant tractors and combines that would more than fill an interstate can be seen roaming the vast fields. Fields so vast that their borders with the freeway seem almost endless, as mile after mile of wheat flashes past on a journey through an otherwise flat and featureless landscape.

Unfortunately, this does tend to make a drive across the state rather monotonous, especially when you no longer have functioning cruise control. Even the workers who painted the white lines on the tarmac seemed to have found it difficult to stay awake on the job; on more than one occasion I saw the painted lane marker veer off towards the shoulder before stopping abruptly, presumably as someone woke with a start.

A convenient chance to break up the journey was presented by Ellis, the boyhood home of Walter P. Chrysler, who in 1925 went on to found the company that bore his name and would in time become one of the 'big three' American car manufacturers.

Ellis, KS, boyhood home of Chrysler founder Walter P. Chrysler.

In 1921, Walter had been hired to help turn around the fortunes of the Willys-Overland Motor Company, originators of the Jeep brand, for which he demanded the unprecedented salary of $1 million. Although Chrysler left the company a couple of years later – taking a few key engineers with him to help set up his own firm – the Chrysler Corporation would reconnect with Jeep when it bought out owners AMC in 1987. The Jeeps Vince and I were driving had both been built in the same town of Toledo, Ohio, that had been the company's home since the Willys days.

I'm sure many wonderful things happened in Kansas the day we were there, but I'm afraid none of them happened to us. To some extent, an uneventful day was just what we needed after the dramas of the first part of our trip. So far we'd nearly been deported, arrested, shunted off the road and sucked into a tornado. A day spent getting our collective heads down and racking up the miles was something of a welcome relief by comparison.

In fact the highlight of our day was nothing more than a routine stop at a Subway just off the interstate, where nothing of any note took place. We received a warm welcome which made up for the still damp and blustery weather, we ate our lunch in peace, refuelled the Jeeps and headed back out on to the road.

In truth, there was a lot to like about Kansas from our perspective. The roads were smooth and well maintained, the rest areas were plentiful, clean and welcoming, and the small number of people we did meet seemed friendly and relaxed, which I took to mean the Kansas way of life agreed with them.

Something that consistently surprised me on this trip was the degree with which the surroundings changed at the border between states. I'd always imagined them to be nothing more than a line drawn hundreds of years ago on some map, probably the result of heated political bartering. And that certainly took place, particularly where it concerned railroad construction or the legality of the slave trade. Other borders shadow the course of a natural or geological feature – the Missouri/Illinois state line, for example, follows the meandering route of the Mississippi River. But even on state lines where nothing obvious emerges to use as a reference, somehow the demarcation presents itself as more than just a small green sign by the side of the road. Sometimes it had included a change in road surface, from concrete to tarmac, while others had arrived with an increase in forestation. The Kansas/Colorado border, however, was far more obvious. It brought with it a change of weather. And another time zone just for good measure.

I'd been looking forward to Colorado. Not just because it allowed me to cheesily say "we're not in Kansas any more" to Vince over the radio. Something about it seemed cool, rugged, independent, and that had always appealed to me.

Named after the Colorado River, it became a part of the Union in 1876, a hundred years after the signing of the Declaration of Independence, thus earning it the nickname of the 'Centennial State.' Geographically, Colorado is something of an over-achiever. It boasts a little of everything from high plains to deserts and snow-capped mountains to deep canyons, and is the only place in the country where four states meet: Colorado, Utah, Arizona and New Mexico.

I've always thought of Colorado as a very forward-thinking place, and since our time there it has gone on to legalise recreational cannabis, decriminalise abortion and assisted suicide, and permit same-sex marriage, even going as far as electing an openly gay governor in 2018.

Even though we drove through Colorado for the best part of two days, this was to be considered just a brief taster; I would return the following week to explore more of this incredible state.

As we arrived on the outskirts of the town of Limon, Vince piped up on the radio.

"We have a choice," he offered. "We have to leave the I-70 here. Now, we could just take the direct route with everyone else. Or we can take the back-road."

"I vote back-road," I replied without hesitation.

I guess I should have been sad about leaving the I-70 behind. It had been our faithful companion for the best part of 1,400 miles and carried us – largely without incident – through eight states. But it was time to leave our tarmac comfort blanket behind, and the prospect of getting into the depths of the countryside was more than a little exciting after so long spent driving in a straight line.

We tanked up the Jeeps and turned off Main Street, rather concerningly following a sign for the local correctional facility. I was just grateful for the change of scenery. We drove past houses with white picket fences decorated with round-topped mailboxes, their little red flags erect. Telegraph poles stretched the length of one side of the road, while edge markers told the story of a road well used to snow cover. Old pickup trucks sat in driveways, as if resting after years of faithful service, while basketball nets hanging from above garage doors hinted at many a Saturday afternoon spent 'shooting hoops.'

We stopped at the side of the road briefly to allow Vince to check his MacGyvered oil catcher. Not a single car passed us while we were parked there. The only sound was that of the Jeeps quietly ticking to themselves as they cooled down.

Crossing the state line earlier that day, a sign had declared: "Welcome to Colorful Colorado!" As if to prove the point, while we stood there at the side of the road the sky filled with such a range of colours we couldn't help but stop what we were doing and stand in awe for a few minutes. Colourful it most certainly was.

With evening upon us we arrived in Colorado Springs, which I will forever remember for the road on which we made a real nuisance of ourselves. Two lanes wide initially, the road rounded a bend and began to climb. Without warning, the right-hand lane – that we happened to be driving in at the time – veered off to the right. Luckily there was just enough room for Vince and I to dive into the remaining lane without upsetting anyone, and that saved us an impromptu excursion into the middle of town, where we may never have been seen again. Once the turning had passed and the right lane reappeared, like good, responsible road users we moved across to allow traffic behind us to pass.

No sooner had we done this but the lane disappeared again, falling away to our right to some unannounced destination without signage or road markings. Again, we slotted ourselves into an available gap in the traffic, but by now we were beginning to upset people. This happened four times. Each time, there was nothing to indicate the lanes would split or where they would go. After the fourth time, Vince and I decided to stay put, holding up traffic until we felt sure we weren't about to be accidentally diverted to God knows where. When finally it felt safe enough to return to the right-hand lane, the angry locals who had been held up behind us sped past, gesticulating and sounding their horns. Quite what we were supposed to do I have no idea, but it remained the most vivid demonstration of how a little signage and some paint can go a long way in road design.

Darkness began to fall as we headed out of town, but we could still make out the outline of the Cheyenne Mountains to our right. The 9,570ft triple peaks are impressive enough, but the area is perhaps most famous as the underground home of NORAD, the North American Aerospace Defense Command. While I will forever associate NORAD with Matthew Broderick's inadvertent attempts to start World War III in *WarGames*, younger generations are more likely to be familiar with NORAD's Santa Tracker, an annual tradition that grew out of a one-off publicity exercise back in 1955.

The contrast in the terrain from the morning could not have been greater. We'd started the day in a tornado and driven in a straight line across hundreds of miles of flat plains. By the evening we found ourselves surrounded by mountain ranges, our route twisting its way through the foothills and scything through cuttings.

We passed through the small town of Florence and followed the signs to our motel, which seemed rather curiously located at the far edge, as if it had been banished by the townspeople. The check-in clerk ran through the procedure almost in slow-motion, and by the time we were finally rewarded with our room keys both Vince and I were too tired to drive back in to town to find somewhere to eat. Instead, we scratched about in the Jeeps for pocket change and shared a bag of Doritos from the motel's vending machines.

It had been another long day. We'd always known the middle section of our trip was likely to be something of a slog, a case of getting our heads down and racking up the miles. But now we were in Colorado the trip had started to take on a different feel. We were no longer driving just to get somewhere.

And tomorrow, we could afford to take our time for once.

CHAPTER SIX

Florence to Moab

025012

C OLORADO MUST BE A GEOLOGIST'S wet dream.
In England, you'd have to drive to somewhere remote and probably legally protected in order to study rock formations in any great detail. But in Colorado, everywhere you look there's a primordial story to be told, one that can be read without leaving the roadside. Great layers of rock strata flashed by as we made our way out of Canon City, their tortured angles alluding to turbulent tales of prehistoric upheaval and creation.

In the far distance, beyond the buildings and civilisation, endless mountain ranges surrounded the view as they rose up towards the grey, watery sky, their peaks obscured by a dampening mist that speckled the Wrangler's windscreen. We were by now more than 5,000ft above sea level, and effectively driving through a cloud.

Highway 50 skirts the edge of Royal Gorge, a six-mile long canyon carved out by the Arkansas River over the course of the last three million years or so. Although 300ft wide at the top, 1,250ft below at its base it measures only 50ft wide, yet it still manages to accommodate the river, a scenic trail known as Tunnel Drive (you can guess why), and the Royal Gorge Route Railroad.

When rich mineral deposits were discovered in the area – particularly silver and lead in what was originally known as Silver City but later renamed to the equally descriptive Leadville – there was a pressing need to build rail access. The Gorge, however, presented something of a natural bottleneck, and when two competing railroad companies both tried to build a line where only one would fit, the result was a two-year struggle that became known as the Royal Gorge War. Court injunctions, armed gangs, sabotage and intimidation, even a 'borrowed' cannon all played their part, but eventually the two sides signed a declaration dubbed the Treaty of Boston and the line was completed in 1880.

Commercial services continued until 1996 when Union Pacific, who had acquired the line through a series of company mergers, finally closed the route. The following year, however, they were encouraged to sell the 12-mile long section through the Gorge so that it could be preserved as a scenic tourist route, and it's been happily shunting suitably vintage rolling stock from Canon City to Parkdale and back since 1999.

Of course, if trains aren't your thing, Royal Gorge also boasts a couple of impressive bridges.

The first, known as the Hanging Bridge, was built in 1878 to carry the railroad through the gorge's narrowest section. At just 30 feet across, the gorge isn't wide enough here to accommodate both the river and the railroad, so an ingenious engineer embedded a series of A-frame girders in the sheer rock walls from which he suspended a 175ft bridge. It's been reinforced over the years but today, over 140 years later, it's still doing its job.

The second is something of a record-breaker. Built in 1929, the Royal Gorge Bridge was the highest in the world until it was usurped in 2001 by a bridge in China, after which it remained the highest suspension bridge until 2003, another title it lost to the Chinese. It's still the highest bridge in America, though, with a 955ft drop to the

The Old West Trading Co. in Royal Gorge, home of cowboy hats, moccasins, carved animals and painted buffaloes.

river below, and at 1,260ft across its span is as long as the Empire State Building is tall. Today it forms the centrepiece in the Royal Gorge Bridge and Amusement Park.

While the more adventurous queued up for white water rafting or the chance to fling themselves into the canyon on a vertigo-inducing zip line, we chose the rather more sedate option of a quick gawp around The Old West Trading Co.

We were initially drawn in by the huge painted buffalo that sat outside the ranch-style building, but lined up next to it was an intriguing army of carved wooden figures – grizzly bears carrying signs preaching visitors to 'wipe yer paws' and intricately detailed two-foot tall cowboys that had evidently 'gone prospectin'.'

As was customary by now, Vince fell into conversation with the proprietor to whom he recounted the story of our road-trip. As the only customers in the shop, we felt duty bound to buy something. I briefly gave serious thought to carrying a three-foot wooden grizzly with me in the Wrangler's passenger seat for the next few weeks. That idea had to be abandoned following the realisation that my new wooden friend would be unlikely to qualify as carry-on luggage. Neither of us felt

sufficiently authentic to pull off the cowboy hat look, but Vince opted instead for a racoon hat. Complete with tail.

I realised I was becoming intolerably infatuated with Colorado. We followed Highway 50 out of Royal Gorge and up through the Arkansas River Canyon where the rock- and tree-covered mountainside nuzzled the edge of the tarmac. To our right, the river continued to carve its way through the canyon, its surface punctuated by huge boulders it had dragged with it for company. We rounded a corner and could hear screaming. Three inflatable rafts bobbed up from beneath the swirling foam, their brightly-attired occupants gasping for breath having survived being simultaneously exhilarated and near-drowned. To the right of the river, the hard-fought-for railroad wound its way around the opposite side of the canyon. Occasionally a freight train appeared, its snake-like body made up not of scales but of fifty or so quarry wagons stretching far into the distance.

I was filled with a feeling that, even today, I find difficult to describe. A sense that anything was possible – the engineering achievements of pioneering settlers, the welcoming sense of fun for modern day trippers – all while preserving the beauty of a landscape that was in equal parts daunting and inspiring. If ever a place epitomised the concept of a 'can do' attitude, this was it. It was like driving through freedom.

Even the colourful Colorado names appealed to me – Bumback Gulch, Bootlegger Gulch, and so on. We pulled off the road into a lay-by (with its own name, no less – Salt Lick Recreation Area – and its own boat ramp) and snapped a few photos of the Jeeps as they glistened against the rocky backdrop. Cotton-wool clouds brushed the tops of the mountains while the river rushed past just a few feet away from us. As Friday mornings went, this was pretty unbeatable.

Just before the small town of Nathrop, we turned off on to the unnamed County Road 162 towards St. Elmo. Towering snow-capped mountains beckoned us from a distance while trees ranged in alternating bands of golden yellows and vibrant reds illuminated our way.

St. Elmo was a mining town founded in 1880 that at its peak was home to around 2,000 people. With almost 150 patented mine claims in the area, the town provided everything the settlers needed – a telegraph office, general store, five hotels, a school house, even a dance hall. The most successful mine, Mary Murphy, produced between 75 and 100 tons of ore a day in 1881, and is estimated to have recovered gold worth almost $60 million over its lifetime. Unfortunately, two fires drove many residents away, while the 1893 repeal of the Sherman Silver Purchase Act (that had artificially inflated the price of silver to one greater even than that of gold) only accelerated its decline. St. Elmo's fate was sealed when the railroad closed in 1922, and although the Mary Murphy mine struggled on until the 1930s, by the 1950s only two full-time residents remained – descendants of the family that had run the town's Home Comfort Hotel. When they finally left in 1958, the town lay abandoned.

St. Elmo's general store, from which you can rent everything from a cabin to an ATV.

Today St. Elmo is one of Colorado's best preserved ghost towns, with many original buildings. One, the general store, opens daily and serves drinks and snacks as well as the chance to rent a cabin or an

ATV. While looking round the store and resisting the chance to buy something else I couldn't fit in hand luggage, Vince and I chatted to the proprietor.

"Let me put a pot of coffee on," he offered, "as there's a very important question I need to ask you."

This sounded a little ominous to me, but he'd been fascinated by the story of our trip so far, so we rolled with it.

"Now. This has puzzled me for years. I've never understood it, and no-one has ever been able to explain it to me. Perhaps you guys, as Brits, could enlighten me."

I was intrigued. Here, in the middle of nowhere, we were about to be quizzed about some deep and meaningful topic that had been troubling this man for heaven knows how long. Perhaps he believed we had somehow stumbled across the meaning of life on our trip, or could answer existential questions about how the Earth came into being. I sipped my coffee and braced myself for whatever question was about to come my way.

He stationed himself back behind the counter and eyed us eagerly.

"What, *exactly*, is a 'lorry?'" he asked.

I was a little taken aback. Perhaps even a touch disappointed at the apparent simplicity of the question, although maybe a little relived in equal measure.

"It's a truck, any kind of goods vehicle, really," we responded.

He pondered this for a moment.

"So, like what we'd call a semi?"

I'd never really thought about the difference between a lorry and a truck before.

"Hmm... not really. We'd call a semi an artic," piped up Vince, careful to pronounce it as 'sem-eye' so as to avoid further confusion. "That's short for 'articulated', a truck where the tractor and trailer are separate." Vince made paddles with his hands as if to illustrate the point. "A lorry is generally a smaller rigid unit, cargo and cab together."

I could see the wheels turning in the proprietor's mind, although I wasn't sure our clarifications were helping.

Agnes Vaille Falls trailhead, now closed after five family members died in a tragic rock fall in 2013.

"So... what's a truck?"

It's easy to see how this can all be so confusing. I rubbed my forehead hoping to stimulate my brain's explanatory powers.

"What you guys call a truck we'd probably think of as a pick-up. And what we'd call a truck could be either a lorry or an artic."

I think by this point we were probably making it worse. It's often been said that Britain and America are two countries divided by a common language. I prayed he didn't ask us to quantify the difference between a bus and a coach.

We took our coffees outside and watched the hyperactive chipmunks that flitted through the log stacks like squirrels on an amphetamine trip.

The sidewalk was made from wooden planks, like so much of the town, and we followed it to the end of what we assumed would once have been called Main Street. Achingly photogenic ramshackle buildings were all around, some sporting mounted deer skulls and other horned trophies.

At the end we found what surely qualified as the world's most pungent pit toilet. Common in remote parts of Colorado, they are largely just as they sound, a deep hole in the ground above which is placed a toilet seat on a pedestal, all housed within a small outhouse. Although rather primitive-sounding in nature, the pit toilets in roadside rest areas are generally clean and well maintained. This one, however, had clearly seen better days. Vince tried his best to relieve himself but, fearing he might be overcome by fumes and inadvertently fall in, never to be seen again, he wisely gave up.

Waved off by the store owner, we climbed back into the Jeeps and returned to the dirt road.

From the roadside, glimpses of bucolic log cabins peeked out from behind the trees, while around every corner appeared a well-serviced campground or trail-head. We pulled in to one – Agnes Vaille Falls. It was named after Denver-born Agnes Wolcott Vaille who served with the American Red Cross in France during World War I, but was perhaps best known locally for her mountaineering exploits. By 1924, she had climbed most of Colorado's 'fourteeners' – that is, mountains with peaks over 14,000ft – no mean feat considering the state has nearly 60 of them, many of which she tackled unaided and in the dead of winter.

In 1925, she set out with Walter Kiener to climb the infamous East Face of Longs Peak, a 1,675ft ascent dominated by a thousand foot sheer cliff known as The Diamond. Having battled gale-force winds and sub-zero temperatures for two days, the pair finally reached the summit. But when the conditions deteriorated further during the return descent, Vaille slipped and fell more than a hundred feet. She survived the fall but was exhausted, her hands and feet frozen. Kiener went on alone to call for help, but when rescuers returned Agnes had died of hypothermia. A stone shelter with a domed roof was built on the spot where she died, while the waterfall was named in her honour by locals.

The conditions had begun to deteriorate for us, too. As I stood in the trail-head parking area trying desperately to do photographic justice to the scene before me, the snow began to fall. We pulled back on to the no-name road, but hadn't travelled more than a few metres before a herd of deer nonchalantly crossed the road in front of us. They seemed wholly unfazed by our presence, almost certainly the least surprised of all America's inhabitants to have come across a pair of right-hand-drive British Jeeps. The last to cross the road was obliging enough to stop and turn to gaze quizzically at us, as if to say "what, haven't you seen a deer cross the road before?"

As Highway 50 carried us further into the mountains, the Jeeps' altitude sickness worsened. We'd re-joined the road at a height of 7,500ft above sea level, but twenty minutes later when we reached the entrance to the Old Monarch Pass, we'd climbed a further 4,000ft. The transmission in Vince's Cherokee seemed to be suffering from the automotive equivalent of hypoxia, and while the Wrangler's cruise control had conked out in Kansas, the Cherokee's had by now failed in sympathy.

"Haven't you seen a deer cross the road before?"

We'd unwittingly driven onto the front of a Christmas card.

The vivid reds and yellows in the treeline had been doused by snow cover, and as we rounded a corner the scene that greeted us was straight off the front of an Alpine Christmas card.

Wranglers don't have outside temperature gauges, but it was clearly well below freezing. The snow crunched into ice beneath our tyres as we pulled in to the rest area at the entrance to Old Monarch Pass to allow the Cherokee's transmission to regain some semblance of sanity.

Monarch Pass used to form part of the original route across the Sawatch mountain range from Gunnison to Poncha Springs. When Highway 50 was built it became *Old* Monarch Pass, but for added interest it connects to Highway 50 either side of the Continental Divide, the notional point at which rivers switch from draining into the Pacific Ocean from the Atlantic.

Today it forms an enticing 15-mile gravel detour that's easily passable in summer but can be treacherous in winter due to ice and a sizeable avalanche risk. Heeding local advice about our lack of snow-chains, we chose not to risk it, but as we went to re-join the highway another motorist who'd stopped in the rest area caught our attention.

Although the roads were clear, immediately off the tarmac lay several inches of snow. The unwary driver of the Ford SUV had strayed just far enough into the powder to make pulling away tricky, particularly given the steep incline. Luckily for him, he found himself

Stopped at the entrance to Old Monarch Pass, just before we had to help the SUV behind us get moving again.

parked behind two qualified off-road instructors, and Vince and I set about feeding him instructions through his open window.

"You *have* got it in four-wheel-drive, right?" Vince queried after our first attempt resulted in little more than wheelspin and a modest slide backwards.

The driver looked at us blankly, and then a realisation grew across his face.

"Actually, I don't know," he said, as he began searching through the various controls. "We've only just bought this, so I'm not sure how everything works yet."

It turned out that when this family had strolled into their local Ford dealer and asked not unreasonably for a 'four wheel drive,' their friendly salesman had interpreted that to mean 'please sell me something you're desperate to get off the lot that looks like an SUV but is actually only two-wheel-drive.'

While Vince and I did finally manage to get them moving again, I like to think they drove straight to their Ford dealer and parked their shiny new non-SUV on top of the salesman's desk.

For the Jeeps, though, it was time to leave Monarch mountain. They'd struggled in the thin air of more than 11,000ft above sea level. By comparison Britain's highest peak, Ben Nevis, is a mere pimple at just 4,411ft. By the time we'd reached Gunnison an hour later we'd dropped to a more sensible 7,700ft, although the Cherokee's transmission if we'd checked would likely have been glowing red at the effort of it all.

Although the view was still bounded by mountain ranges, the flatter terrain gave rise to farms and ranches on the outskirts of town. The changes in altitude, however, had had an unwelcome effect on my bladder. We resolved to stop at the first eatery that appeared in an attempt to be more adventurous with our eating habits. Unfortunately for us, that turned out to be a McDonald's. Complete with flooded toilets.

Highway 50 out of Gunnison is, frankly, a petrolhead's dream, with its smooth tarmac, sinuous curves and beautiful scenery. As the sun began to project its golden hues on to us from behind the mountain ranges, the Gunnison River opened out to something more akin to an inland sea. We might have been in the least performance-oriented vehicles possible but we were still capable of enjoying the drive. In fact, my love affair with Colorado only deepened when I decided it was probably worth the 8-hour flight and 2,000-mile road-trip just so we could drive this road. I made Vince stop in a rest area just so I could prolong the moment, at least partly because I knew this leg of our trip was nearly over. I didn't know it at the time, but Vince was quietly hatching a plan that would see us arrive in Moab a day early.

From this point, we could have taken things easy. Perhaps a leisurely drive into the next town, a quiet meal somewhere interesting, and an overnight stay in any one of a number of motels along the way. Instead, Vince's excitement got the better of him. He looked at his satnav and saw that, in its trouble- and traffic-free world, we were only three hours or so from Moab. That ought to be easily achievable in what remained of the evening, right?

That's how we found ourselves racing through Montrose, sprinting through Delta, and utterly and hopelessly lost in Grand Junction.

Highway 50 out of Gunnison River was so littered with sinuous curves that it was almost worth the trip by itself.

Three hours became four. Four hours became five. And then, just as I was contemplating hooking up some kind of intravenous Red Bull drip, Vince's Cherokee caught fire.

Vince isn't prone to making sudden, unplanned manoeuvres, so when the Cherokee swung wildly off I-70 and on to a side road, I knew something was wrong. As the Jeep turned I could see the windows were open and, for a brief moment, I thought I could smell burning.

"What's up, Vince?" I called out over the radio.

There was no response.

The Cherokee ground to a halt at the side of the road and its tail-lights went out. I pulled the Wrangler up a safe distance from it, hit the hazard lights and leapt out. I could smell the unmistakably pungent aroma of burning plastic and as I reached the driver's window I could see Vince was pulling fuses, coughing furiously. I grabbed the driver's door and Vince jumped out, taking a lung-full of unpolluted air as he did.

"What happened?" I asked, peering in through the open rear windows for any obvious clues. I could see Vince had somehow lifted the rear carpets, exposing the wiring beneath.

"Electrical fire," Vince gasped between breaths.

A key principle in off-road driving, particularly in rocky environments such as those found in Moab, is that of reducing the air pressure inside the vehicle's tyres. More colloquially known as 'airing down' this increases the amount of surface area the tyre has in contact with the ground and also allows the tyre to deform around a rock, effectively grasping it as you might with your hand. Naturally this requires re-inflating the tyres before returning to the tarmac, so many off-road prepared vehicles include what's known as 'on-board air' – a compressor secreted away somewhere that can be used to quickly return the tyres to their regular street pressure.

Vince's Cherokee carries a modest compressor mounted in a recess in the boot, a location that necessitates the running of a 12-volt line from the engine compartment through the cabin. As it turned out, the wiring supplied with the compressor wasn't man enough for the job, and over the course of the last 2,000 miles the heat from the exhaust beneath the floor had been enough to melt the insulation creating a short circuit and starting a small fire. Vince's quick thinking at pulling the fuses and lifting the carpet, all while driving down the interstate,

The offending rear-mounted air compressor.

saved his Jeep from a fiery end. Now all we had to do was wait for the acrid stench of melted plastic and singed carpet to dissipate.

Keen to make up time, we re-joined our old friend the I-70 and pressed on. Darkness had fallen some hours ago, but I could still make out the features that lay behind so much of Colorado's beauty. Black mountain ranges were silhouetted against an inky blue, moonlit sky, while jutting rock formations flashed by, picked out of the gloom by the Jeeps' headlights.

One feature caught by our lights was less welcome, however. A sign by the side of the road, echoing one we'd seen the day before, said simply: "Leaving colorful Colorado." I'd loved my time in Colorado, and over the last two days it had become strangely familiar, homely even. Leaving it behind felt like abandoning a favourite pair of Timberland boots. The appearance of a sign depicting Arches National Park and declaring "Welcome to Utah" was, at the time, scant consolation.

Vince had been telling me for days about how impressive the drive into Moab would be, with its red rock cliffs and towering plateaus, but all my headlights could lift out of the darkness was what looked like desert scrub by the roadside. Following the almost arrow-straight Highway 191 south into Moab, there were no signs of civilisation, no lights burning brightly in the distance, and no landmarks against which to measure our progress. The only reference point I had was the back of Vince's Cherokee and the few feet of painted lane markings I could see in front of the Wrangler.

Soon after crossing the bridge into Moab the familiar elevated Super 8 sign of our motel appeared. This was to be our home for the next two weeks or so, but as we drove around the packed car park looking for spaces, a realisation dawned somewhere in the Cherokee. In Vince's excitement to get to Moab, he'd overlooked one very important fact: our reservations weren't until tomorrow. Moab is the ultimate destination for many, and it's not unusual for every motel in town to be fully booked months in advance. We explained our predicament to the motel staff, but there was nothing they could do – they were full. The staff in the Motel 6 down the road told us that as far as they knew, everywhere in town was fully booked. It was beginning to look like we'd driven all this way just to spend the night in the Jeeps.

We sought refuge in the familiarity of the Denny's diner next door, grateful for their warm welcome. While chatting to the waitress, we recounted our sob story – we'd driven nearly 2,500 miles and now, due to our own stupidity, had nowhere to stay.

"Have you tried Red Cliffs Lodge?" she suggested. "It's a bit out of town and probably very expensive, but they might have something."

"Of course, I didn't think of that," replied Vince, who'd been to Moab before and evidently knew where she was talking about.

"If you don't have any luck, remember we're open 24 hours. You're welcome to spend it with us. We serve great pie!"

She was right, they do. We polished off the piece we'd ordered, downed our coffee, and climbed back into the Jeeps.

Red Cliffs Lodge is a twenty minute Jeep ride out of town along an unnamed road that hugs the edge of the Colorado River. Not that we could see it in the darkness, of course, but we could certainly hear it.

Occasionally a boulder or two was picked out by the headlights, but otherwise there was little to give away much about the terrain we were driving through.

The Lodge appeared out of nowhere, a ranch styled very much in the wild west theme, with the added bonus of its own winery, movie museum and stabling. We ventured tentatively into reception, aware that it was by now well into the small hours of the morning. The night porter announced that, yes, he had an empty cabin and he'd be happy to let us stay in it for a mere $200. At this point I think both Vince and I were too tired to realise that this was more than four times what we'd been used to paying, so we accepted, gladly. We followed his directions to our cabin, parked the Jeeps outside what looked like our own private ranch complete with veranda, and dragged our bags inside. This was when we discovered our two hundred bucks had only bought us one bed.

Admitting that our early arrival in town without so much as a reservation had technically been his fault, Vince administered his own self-punishment by spending the night on the freezing cold fold-out sofa bed.

CHAPTER SEVEN

Moab

`02601`

F OR THE FIRST TIME IN a week, we had no particular place to be other than here. I'd been awake for some time, but had been determined to lay in bed for a while just because I could. When Vince began to stir on his sofa bed, I pulled on some clothes and drew back the curtains.

"Wow."

There really was no other word for it.

Red Cliffs Lodge isn't named after someone called Cliff, nor is it red. Instead, the name comes from the fact it sits between a series of enormous red rock cliffs, rising up behind our cabin like a giant wall from some alien world. They'd been completely hidden during our drive here the night before, making the view from our cabin's terrace that morning even more breath-taking.

I could see horses grazing contentedly in the fields beyond, while all around was a stillness, a quiet sense of calm that signalled a welcome change of pace given the hectic mile-munching itinerary we'd been subject to over the last few days. I loved Colorado, and was sad to

Our cabin at Red Cliffs Lodge was surrounded by a Martian landscape.

leave it behind. But it was clear Moab and I were going to be good friends.

We checked out of our cabin, loaded the Jeeps, and headed back into town. The road to Moab could not have appeared more different now to how it seemed the night before. It scythed its way from one corner to the next, hemmed in by the Colorado River on one side and towering sheer cliff walls that came right up to the tarmac edge on the other. Yesterday this was just a road in the middle of nowhere; today it was like driving through a canyon on the surface of Mars.

We rounded a corner and had to swerve to avoid a group of climbers, dangling at windscreen height from the cliff face as it jutted out high above us. Their car was parked just a few yards away and I remember wondering how many places in the world provided the opportunity to park up and start climbing without having to take another step.

The town of Moab sits within a plateau, and although early settlers used it as an important crossing point over the Colorado River, it wasn't until 1902 that it became officially incorporated. Its agricultural economy shifted during the 1950s when rich uranium deposits were discovered, earning it the title of the 'Uranium Capital of the World.'

During this time the population grew to almost 6,000 but with the end of the Cold War many homes stood empty by the 1980s.

Hollywood perhaps did more to cement Moab's place in popular culture after John Ford was persuaded to film *Wagon Master* here in 1949. Many a John Wayne western used Canyonlands and Arches National Park as backdrops, as have modern classics from *Indiana Jones* to *Star Trek*. More recently it's been the location for Emmy-winning series *Westworld*.

Since 1967 it's been home to the Easter Jeep Safari which, despite the name, brings together off-roaders, mountain bikers, hikers and others for nine days of sheer unbridled outdoorsyness.

What struck me as we drove down Main Street was how clean everything seemed. Green, too, with well-tended verges and freshly-watered grass – not what you might expect in what is effectively an arid desert.

Outnumbering the drive-through banks and coffee huts by some margin was a vast array of businesses offering everything from Jeep and

Moab sits within a plateau, surrounded by red cliffs and snow-capped mountains.

The rocks really are that red; it feels more like a film set.

ATV rental to mountain bikes, canoes, and tours of every conceivable kind. For the people who brought their adventure with them, there were repair shops and outfitters for every activity you could think of.

Again, I found myself filled with the same sense of positivity I'd felt in Colorado. Back home in the UK, different user groups seem determined to organise themselves into narrow-minded fiefdoms, permanently at war with everyone else. As a 4x4 driver, I'd often found myself at the pointy end of a misinformed rant delivered by a red-faced rambler. Off-roaders have access to less than 1% of the UK's byway network, but despite being more heavily involved in repair work and trail maintenance than any other group, there are still those that will not rest until 4x4s are banned altogether. Yet here in Moab it was clear that hikers, trail riders, quad-bikers and Jeepers were all capable of co-existing and sharing the same incredible terrain.

We swung the Jeeps into Smitty's parking lot and headed inside for breakfast. Pancakes – what else? While we chose from the overly elaborate selection of toppings and avoided pouring coffee over anything we shouldn't, we made a mental list of the things we needed to achieve that day. Top of the list was to find a muffler shop that could build a new rear exhaust for Vince's Cherokee, as Clayton's system was rather too loud and almost certainly not UK-legal.

We found a shop on the edge of town, appropriately enough named Moab 4x4 Outpost, that seemed a likely candidate. Steve, the proprietor, came up with a plan that incorporated everything Vince wanted, and we made a booking to leave the Cherokee with him in a few days' time so he could take care of it.

Now that we actually had reservations, we checked in to our Super 8 motel and dumped our belongings in our rooms. We were free. We didn't have to be anywhere in particular, we had no deadlines, and we were in Moab with two well-prepared Jeeps. And unlike most foreigners that visit Moab for a 4x4 adventure, they weren't rental Jeeps – they were our own.

We spread a trail map out across the bonnet of the Cherokee and picked out a route on which we could test the Jeeps. Heading up to Canyonlands National Park, we opted for a section of White Rim Road before using Shafer Trail to link up with Potash Road. Since we'd end

The Colorado River forms endless loops through the rocky landscape.

up close by, we'd swing by Dead Horse Point to take in the incredible view.

It's impossible to overstate how other-worldly Moab feels. Vivid red boulders were piled high at the side of the trail, as if placed there by some giant intergalactic park ranger, while elsewhere beneath the red dust lay flat rocks of brilliant blue. It was hard not to feel like we'd inadvertently strayed onto the set of *Forbidden Planet.*

The trail wound a precarious course along the edge of a rocky rim, cloud-stopping peaks to one side, sheer drops to the other. At Thelma & Louise Point – named after the movie which saw Susan Sarandon and Geena Davis drive off the edge, and not the Grand Canyon as you might think – the trail passes within just a few feet of a precipitous drop to the Colorado River below.

As the river winds its way through the deep canyons it forms endless loops and kinks, on the banks of which green vegetation makes its home, softening the otherwise rocky edges that dominate the landscape. Where the trail brushed past the river, we stood on an outcrop and tried to comprehend the scale of what stretched out before us.

From here, Shafer Trail writhes its way up a 1,500ft cliff face through a series of hairpins and switchbacks. Many an enthusiastic driver has heard of the Stelvio Pass on the Italian/Swiss border; Shafer Trail is perhaps the off-road equivalent. An old mining trail, the five-mile route can be driven by any well-equipped four-wheel-drive vehicle, although its rock-strewn surface can easily catch out the inexperienced or those with limited ground clearance. In places the trail is only just wide enough for one vehicle; blind bends can make it difficult to spot oncoming traffic, leading to a heart-stopping reversing manoeuvre. It's worth it, though. The views from the top are breath-taking, while the *Island in the Sky* visitor centre does an excellent job of explaining some of the geology of the area.

We pushed on to Dead Horse Point. Legend has it that it was used as a natural corral by early cowboys to hold wild mustangs to be broken. Those that weren't selected were left to find their own way back to

the open range, but one story suggests a band of 'broomtails' refused to leave the point, eventually dying of thirst within sight of the river 2,000ft below. Today it forms the start point of many biking, hiking and camping spots, all with stunning views out across the canyons, the Technicolor potash evaporation ponds beyond, and on to the snow-capped La Sal mountain range.

As a test, our scenic excursion had worked perfectly. Our list of required remedial work grew slightly after we discovered the Wrangler's suspension control arms were hitting the exhaust at times, while the Cherokee's exhaust – already set to be replaced in the coming days – had been denting the rear shock absorbers.

For our journey back to Moab we opted to stay off-road and take Long Canyon Road, primarily so we could drive through Pucker Pass. Pucker factor is a principle well known to off-roaders. It has little to do with puckering one's lips and far more to do with the involuntary tightening of one's sphincter when tackling a particularly challenging or scary obstacle. Pucker Pass involves squeezing under a house-sized rock that fell across the trail, and although it's been there for years, the precarious angle it now rests at creates the feeling it may, at any time, slip and crush an unwary adventurer.

The trail ends where Highway 279 follows the banks of the Colorado River, and from there a three-mile section has become known as 'Wall Street.' Not because there's a row of banks there and not, as I liked to think, because it's home to a family of geckos all named Gordon. Instead its name comes from the sheer cliffs that rise 1,000ft up from the roadside like a giant wall. Popular with climbers and equipped with rest areas and camp grounds, it's also one of the easiest places to see ancient Native American petroglyphs. Attributed to the Fremont culture and likely to have been carved into the rock more than a thousand years ago, they depict both human and animal figures, although no-one seems certain of their exact meaning. They are remarkably well preserved, their height of 15ft or more above the road surface having helped them to escape damage from more modern graffiti.

Ancient petroglyphs, carved perhaps more than a thousand years ago, easily visible from the road side.

After a quick shower in our motel rooms (that red Moab dust gets everywhere), we left the Jeeps behind and walked into town – easier said than done in a country that expects you to drive everywhere and often doesn't provide sidewalks. More than once a passing police car slowed down to eye us cautiously, fearing we were up to no good.

We'd arranged to meet up with friends in Eddie McStiff's bar (no, it's really called that), and it was here that we discovered Utah's unfathomable alcohol laws. We'd tried to order beers at the bar, but the barman seemed to be on commission from the kitchen.

"You gotta eat," he said, shaking his head.

"But we've already eaten, we just want a beer," we replied.

I looked around and could see plenty of people nursing bottles of beer and glasses of wine. None of them seemed to be eating.

"No food, no beer." He clearly wasn't budging.

"Alright," I relented, "let's have some nachos to share. Good enough?"

This seemed to make the barman happier.

"Sure," he said, handing us two unopened beer bottles.

I found a table I liked the look of and we sat down, wearily. I was about to twist the cap off my bottle when a passing waitress stopped me.

"You can't sit here!" she screamed.

This was all about to become incredibly confusing. There was no reserved sign on the table, and nothing to indicate it was different to any other.

"Why not?" I asked, more than a little perplexed.

"You've got no food!" she exclaimed, as if it were the most obvious thing in the world.

"We've ordered food. We've sat down to wait for it."

"But you can't sit here!"

Fearing this conversation could literally go on until the end of time, I stood up, just to stop her from telling me not to sit there any more.

"Look, I just want to drink my beer. We've ordered food, but it isn't here yet. If we can't sit here, where *can* we sit?"

She pointed at an identical table directly opposite the one I'd been evicted from.

"You can sit here," she said, with precisely zero irony.

Fearing the explanation as to why might take the rest of my natural life, I sat down without another word. My confusion levels were about to go through the roof, however. As the waitress turned to leave, she left us with a parting shot.

"When your food arrives, you can go back to the other table."

Vince and I stared at each other in complete bewilderment. We knew the Mormon state had some fairly arcane alcohol laws, but this was beyond anyone's comprehension.

Our nachos arrived. At least, I think they did – a waitress deposited a small basket in the middle of the table which seemed to contain nothing but melted cheese. I imagined our nachos were concealed underneath, but I had little enthusiasm for lifting the greasy blanket to find out. I picked up our slime-laden basket and carried it across to our preferred table, fearing we might be barked at if we didn't move back.

Through the course of the evening we tried many of the locally-brewed beers, some of which were 'infused' (their words, not mine) with other flavours such as lime and raspberry. This was a mistake, and for several reasons.

Firstly, Moab sits at an elevation of just over 4,000ft above sea level and conventional wisdom suggests this has an effect on your body's tolerance for alcohol. Secondly, making an alcoholic drink that tastes sweet and innocent only makes it easier to knock back, although perhaps that's exactly why they did it.

But lastly, it was a mistake because my friend Vince is famous for his low alcohol tolerance. Part way through his second beer, he declared he had an instant hangover and wanted to go home. Since home was by that time more than five thousand miles away, I suggested he used the McBasket o' Slime to soak up some of the alcohol in his stomach and give the fruit-infused beers a miss for a while.

Our ability to walk in a straight line seemed even more important when I remembered our route back to our motel lacked a sidewalk and neither of us had thought to bring a flashlight.

~

Vince appeared to have survived the night without serious organ damage, if the rate at which he tucked into his morning pancakes was anything to go by.

We had a rather unusual day ahead of us. For the first time since landing in America, we were about to be Jeepless.

We drove the Jeeps back to Moab 4x4 Outpost and left them with Steve, the proprietor, to address the various niggles we'd uncovered during our previous day's testing. Most of Steve's efforts would concentrate on reworking the exhausts to fix clearance issues. The Cherokee would gain a custom fabricated rear muffler and have its over-axle pipework re-shaped slightly, while the Wrangler's more

Steve had fitted a custom set-up with very little room to play with.

complicated set-up would have to wait until we returned to the UK before it could be resolved properly. For now, we asked Steve to cut off much of the Wrangler's rear system and add a turn-down just beyond the transfer case. This had the added bonus of making the Wrangler sound like a Mustang, but would seriously upset the UK authorities and so could only be considered temporary.

Without the Jeeps, we were a little lost. We wandered into town for a spot of that uncharacteristically male past-time of 'shopping,' although given we were in Moab we seemed to spend a disproportionate amount of time in shops selling things like winches, hiking gear, and mountain bikes. We managed to resist the urge to buy something difficult to explain like a quad bike, settling instead for a handful of T-shirts, all featuring images of Utah – sunrise over Arches National Park, Jeeps ascending Lion's Back, and so on.

I borrowed Vince's laptop and spent the afternoon in my motel room sorting through the hundreds of photos I'd taken on the trip so far, until Steve called to say the Jeeps were ready. We might have only been separated from them for a day, but it was surprising how strange that felt. Having spent every waking hour in them since we landed, having shared so many experiences, perhaps it was only natural that we should become so attached to them. Even now as I write these words it sounds ridiculous to suggest that such a bond should be capable of forming between man and machine. I even found myself wondering if the Wrangler had missed me. Would we arrive at the Outpost only to be told by Steve that the Jeeps had refused to start, like naughty children determined to misbehave in protest at being left with a babysitter?

Thankfully in the end Steve hadn't been subjected to any such mischief, and other than finding it "weird" driving from the passenger seat when moving the Jeeps into the workshop, he'd had no difficulty in taking care of our snagging list.

With the Jeeps safely tucked up in our motel parking lot, we wandered back into town to meet up with friends at Pasta Jay's. Now something of a Moab institution, as the name suggests this place is all about the pasta. And pizza. Oh, and fabulous meatball sandwiches. We gathered together in a clump under the heated veranda, where we probably made too much noise and almost certainly ate too much pizza.

CHAPTER EIGHT

Top of the World

02683♫

PART OF THE JUSTIFICATION FOR going to the effort of shipping our Jeeps across the Atlantic, essentially re-engineering them, and then nearly having them confiscated in Philadelphia by angry cops, was so that we could spend our time in Moab driving our own off-roaders, rather than having to resort to hiring one like everyone else. Not that there's anything wrong with that as such, but it can be rather limiting.

While most rental outlets tend to hire out completely standard Jeeps, there are some that will gladly offer you a Wrangler with a few modest modifications – perhaps a two-inch suspension lift, two inch taller tyres, and so on. Two inches might not sound like much, but that's enough to open up a whole range of trails that are inaccessible to a standard vehicle. But it doesn't open all of them.

To tackle trails like Steel Bender, Behind the Rocks, or Strike Ravine, requires something a little more specialised. Perhaps, say, a Cherokee with an eight-inch lift, a Wrangler with a 5½-inch lift, and 35-inch tyres all round?

That's all well and good for Vince and I, since that's what we brought with us. But for our friends who'd flown out to Utah to join us, we wanted to give them their own taste of the Moab experience. Cliffhanger Jeep Rental were happy to oblige with a small army of Wranglers with modest suspension lifts and All Terrain tyres. All we needed now was a suitable trail.

The Top of the World trail climbs for ten miles or so over a series of rocky ledges and shelves until it reaches its 7,000ft summit, from which are promised endless views out across Fisher Valley, Onion Creek and the La Sal mountains.

It starts just off Highway 128 where a new bridge takes over from the now-ruined Dewey Suspension Bridge. Built in 1916, it was designed to support the weight of six horses, three wagons and 9,000 pounds of freight, and was a vital route for trade and supplies across the Colorado River. Although a ferry had previously offered a crossing service, the Dewey bridge was the first direct connection, and even to this day it remains Utah's longest suspension bridge. Sadly, the wooden deck was destroyed by fire in 2008 by a six-year-old boy playing with matches, and although a certain degree of enthusiasm exists for its restoration, today its metal towers stand naked as the steel cables swing forlornly in the breeze.

The trail starts easily enough with a well graded sand and gravel track, but soon after turning into the trailhead the terrain becomes much more interesting. The rocky ledges require careful thought about tyre placement, and it's important to choose a line through each obstacle that accommodates both the skill of the driver and the capability of the vehicle. Most of our party were experienced off-roaders, and while a showroom-fresh four-wheel-drive would likely be stopped in its tracks by some of the harder obstacles, our Jeeps were perfectly matched.

The appeal of off-roading is different for everyone. For some it's the challenge, the reward in the sense of achievement of traversing terrain that at first glance often looks impossible. For others, it's the chance to escape the modern world, to seek out adventure literally

in the middle of nowhere. Not for nothing has Jeep spent the last 70 years hanging their marketing on the concept of freedom. And it's hard to imagine how anyone without access to a 4x4 would ever get to see the incredible sights Utah laid on for us that day.

Unfortunately, fate is not without a sense of irony. Having gone to all the effort of getting Vince's Cherokee here, it broke an upper shock absorber mount on the way up the trail, forcing Vince to stay behind and effect a repair while we pushed on to the summit.

More irony arrived in the guise of a group of Land Rovers ascending the trail behind us. After shipping our American Jeeps all the way from England, here we were being chased by a group of British-built Discoverys from America.

As it turned out, the Top of the World trail is well named. The trail ends on a giant inclined slab of rock, and it's not until you peer at it from the side that you realise part of it juts out over the canyon. None of our party felt brave enough (or sufficiently insured, frankly) to park a Jeep on the edge for the obligatory photo, so instead we marvelled at the 360-degree views. Before us – but 2,000ft below – lay Fisher Valley, through which could just be made out the easy-rated Onion

Creek trail as it wound its way through the crumpled terrain. Beyond that, the far edge of the valley rose out of the ground like an elevating plateau, while on the horizon the La Sal mountains drew the eye with their sugar-coated peaks. To our right Fisher Towers, popular with climbers for their corkscrew summit, stood out from the surrounding formations as they reached up towards us, while behind us the horizon seemed to climb ever skyward – partly due to the disorienting sloping plateau we were standing on, and partly due to the Book Cliffs that stretch for 200 miles across the Colorado/Utah border.

We left the Land Rovers to take our place at the summit and retraced our tracks, collecting Vince and the now fixed Cherokee, and convoyed our way back towards Moab.

Our plan for the afternoon after a quick lunch stop and the chance to use some thankfully less pungent pit toilets, was to lead the group through Fins 'n' Things. Part of the Sand Flats Recreation Area, the 'fins' were originally sand dunes that over the course of 200 million years cemented themselves into sandstone, while the 'things' are what remains as the fins erode naturally over time, effectively returning to their original state.

Although a geologist would probably refer to it as sandstone, in Moab and in Jeep circles in particular it's more likely to be known as 'slickrock.' Rather confusingly, there's nothing slick about it. In fact, with rubber tyres there's so much traction that it's more akin to driving on very coarse sandpaper. Instead the term was coined by early settlers whose horses' metal shoes and metal-ringed wagon wheels had difficulty gaining purchase, and so the name stuck.

The trail itself is just over nine miles long, its route through the rocky terrain marked by painted dinosaur symbols. There are stiff fines for anyone venturing off-piste, with the Bureau of Land Management even having the power to confiscate offenders' vehicles.

From the very start, the omnipresent La Sal mountains dominated the horizon, and while I stood at the top of a rocky ridge to photograph a posing Wrangler, I could feel the snow-chilled air as it rolled off their peaks towards us.

The cold air could be felt rolling off the snow-capped peaks towards us.

Much of the trail consists of short 50-degree climbs followed by up to 70-degree descents on the other side, some with off-camber ledges thrown in for good measure. Other parts require traversing along the top of a narrow ridge, following the tyre tracks left by those that have gone before you, and descending under engine braking to control your speed.

Several steeper climbs require careful technique. As the front wheels start the ascent the windscreen fills with sky, robbing you of any point of reference. It's here that a good 'spotter' – someone outside the vehicle calling out instructions to guide you – becomes worth their weight in gold. Power needs to be applied just before the rear wheels meet the obstacle; too late, and the Jeep won't make the climb. Too little power and the result will be nothing more than four tyres chirping against the slickrock and a Jeep going nowhere fast. Too much and the Jeep could roll over backwards, very quickly ruining everyone's day. Thankfully there were no such dramas for us that day, although a few of our group experienced more than their fair share of teetering moments.

As the sun dipped below the horizon a warm glow rose up from behind the mountains, signalling it was time to return the rental Jeeps. After a hot day on the trails we were beginning to crave some cold refreshment. And with that thought, the convoy sprinted its way back to Moab in the hope we'd make it back before the ice cream parlour closed.

CHAPTER NINE

San Juan Skyway

03186🔁

OAB IS AN AWE-INSPIRING PLACE, but it should be
no secret by now that I loved Colorado. Should I ever be
consumed by the desire to relocate, Colorado, without a
doubt, is where I'd move to. When Vince and I drove across it a week
ago, I'd vowed to return as soon as the chance presented itself. And
with Vince now busy with other commitments for the next few days,
this seemed the perfect opportunity.

During the prep for our trip before leaving England, I'd come across
something called the San Juan Skyway. Part of the Colorado Scenic
and Historic Byway system, the 238-mile loop passes over the San Juan
Mountains, linking up with a series of historic towns in the process.
When the route plan announced it incorporated something called the
Million Dollar Highway, I was sold.

With a full tank of gas and a printed copy of the route, I followed
the 191 south out of Moab on my own. It seemed strange to not be
staring at the back of Vince's Cherokee any more. Now I was on a
more primitive road-trip; it was just me and the open road.

Spruce Tree House is tucked into a natural alcove.

Highway 191 picked its route carefully through Utah's Martian terrain, winding through valleys and turning to avoid rock formations that appeared out of nowhere, as if they'd landed there from outer space. Where they proved unavoidable, the road passed through a wide channel sliced through them, leaving a small outcrop to one side that looked lost and forlorn. As I drew closer to Monticello, a towering plateau rose up before me and the road began its inexorable thousand foot climb. The Blue Mountains dominated the horizon to my right, much like the La Sal mountains had done in Moab, and I turned left onto Highway 491 towards Cortez. It was here that I very nearly had a serious accident.

It was my own stupid fault. Leaving Highway 491 behind, I moved across into the centre turn lane, a filter lane in the middle of the road for cars turning against oncoming traffic, and waited for my chance to turn left. It was a manoeuvre I'd performed countless times before, and other than some large concrete dividers and the roads being at a strange angle to each other, there was nothing special about this one. But for some reason only having to watch traffic moving in one direction seemed to recalibrate my brain, and when I arrived at a crossroads a hundred yards later, fifteen years of driving experience suddenly abandoned me. I needed to drive straight across a very busy Main Street, but my brain had decided this was a one way road and I only needed to wait for a gap in traffic coming from my left. Since there didn't seem to be any traffic from my right, what little remained of my brain after most of it had apparently jumped out the window didn't see anything wrong with this. And so, I dutifully waited until a gap in traffic appeared, and I sauntered casually across the road.

I cleared the crossroads and glanced in my rear-view mirror – and saw a huge truck barrel past me, mere inches from my back bumper, travelling in the opposite direction. The realisation dawned.

'What have I just done!?'

'You've just driven across four lanes of traffic without bothering to check both ways, you bloody idiot!'

I couldn't believe it. I pulled over to the side of the road and sat for a moment, replaying the last few seconds of my life, grateful that I still could. If I'd pulled away a second later, or a touch slower, I'd have been T-boned by a speeding truck. Chances are I'd be dead, or at least have a Peterbilt engine embedded in my head, neither of which are likely to be a good look for anyone.

It was some time before I felt I could continue, but even today that incident replays itself in my mind as a reminder to be more careful. Thankfully, it was the only such incident during my time in America.

The first leg of the skyway from Cortez towards Durango passes right by the entrance to Mesa Verde and, having always wanted to piece together a road-trip of America's national parks, I couldn't possibly drive past now without stopping.

Mesa Verde is home to nearly 5,000 archaeological sites of the Ancestral Pueblo people who lived in the area for more than 700 years until around 1300 AD. Established in 1906, the park is perhaps most famous for its 600 or so cliff dwellings, some of the best preserved in the country.

Whereas the UK's idea of a national park is a few rolling hills with strict building regulations and the odd gravel car park, in America a national park is a fearsomely organised thing. Entrances are manned by welcoming and knowledgeable rangers, while a visitor centre tells the story of the park through easy-to-understand displays. Its staff happily dispense a series of printed guides to accompany your visit, each marking out the park's highlights, the best viewpoints and where to have a pee without scaring the wildlife. Everything is well signed and well maintained, but perhaps the most impressive aspect is how accessible it all is.

Given the 'drive-thru' nature of much of America this perhaps shouldn't be so surprising, but like most parks Mesa Verde boasts a network of roads carefully arranged in a loop around the most impressive sights. Visitors need only drive from one parking area to the next, from which a walk of often just a few yards reveals a spectacular viewpoint across the park's 52,000 acres, or down into a natural alcove and an ancient cliff dwelling. The largest – Cliff Palace – has over 150 rooms and is thought to have been home to around 100 people.

I parked up at the first viewpoint and followed the steep and winding footpath down into a canyon. There, a 216ft wide alcove provided the natural shelter for Spruce Tree House. Formed from rough-hewn sandstone bricks, some of its 130 rooms were square, others were round, while some descended into the cave floor, but each had its own purpose. I stood there for a while, trying to imagine what it might have been like to live there, before heading back up the steep trail.

Thoughtfully placed bench seats gave the opportunity to rest a moment during the ascent, and perched on one I came across an elderly couple enjoying a breather.

"Looks like you've found a nice spot," I called out as a friendly, throw-away greeting as I walked past.

The man looked at me with stern surprise, like I'd just insulted his wife. People, I'd found, are normally friendly in these situations if you go to the trouble of making the effort. But maybe I'd just found the exception.

His face scrunched into an all-pervading squint and he fixed me with his narrowing eyes.

"Where are you from, then?" he asked.

"I'm from England," I answered, once again fearing I sounded like a *Mary Poppins* character who'd become hopelessly lost.

His face softened as gradually his scrunched-up features opened up like a hedgehog unfurling itself, and he launched himself back on to his feet.

"Gee, I love England," he said. "I used to live there, you know."

"Really?" The world truly is a small place.

"Yeah, I did my teacher training there, after the war." His eyes were glinting with excitement; this was clearly his favourite topic of conversation.

"Oh, what did you teach?"

"English." I probably should have guessed that. "I've been an English teacher ever since," he elaborated proudly.

"That's amazing. Are you still teaching now?"

"No, I retired just a few years ago. We bought a Winnebago and now my wife and I spend our time travelling around the country. Here," he said, motioning along the steep path, "I'll walk with you. You can tell me what brings *you* here."

I started to recount the story of our trip, but after we'd walked a few paces I stopped and turned to look back towards the man's wife, still sitting on the bench.

"Shouldn't we wait for your wife?" I asked. He paused to consider the question.

"She'll find her own way up when she's ready," he said.

I felt guilty leaving her behind. I wanted to offer her an arm to help her up the steep trail, but the man was already striding off up the canyon. Eventually she left the safety of the bench and started shuffling her way up towards us. As the man and I talked, I could hear her puffing away behind us but each time I turned to make sure she was OK, the man asked a question to distract me. I couldn't help but form the impression of a rather quiet, perhaps lonely atmosphere

inside the Winnebago as it toured its way across America, and that this might have been the first time the man had had a conversation with another person in weeks.

When we reached the top I thanked the man for his company and was about to return to the car park. The man looked dejected, perhaps even a little offended that I was about to end our time together. I held up my camera and asked if I could take his picture as a memento. He declined, but insisted he used it to take a picture of me. With that complete, I held out my hand.

"It's been nice chatting," I said.

"It has," he replied, shaking my hand vigorously. "You take care now on the rest of your trip."

However long I spent at Mesa Verde I sensed I would only ever be scratching the surface. A small sign appeared at the side of the road pointing rather nondescriptly towards something called Park Point. The road was narrow and clearly ignored by most travellers, but on a whim I decided to follow it. Naked twisted branches of long-burnt bushes lined the side of the road, while at their base the green foliage of rejuvenation began to take hold. Eventually, the road terminated at a deserted parking lot, from which a steep but well-paved walking trail took over. At its summit, a small ranger station looked out across the park, presumably as a fire look-out, while a small sign declared that this was the highest point in Mesa Verde at 8,572ft. The views seemed to be endless, obscured only where mountains or plateaus rose up to meet the horizon. It's said that on a clear day, the views stretch as far as the point where the four states of Utah, Arizona, Colorado and New Mexico meet, roughly 40 miles away.

Conscious of the speed with which time was slipping away from me, I tore myself away from the scenery and re-joined Highway 160.

I could never tire of driving through Colorado. The road writhed its way through the mountains, bucking and twisting with the changing contours, endlessly adapting to the prevailing elevation. Hillsides carpeted with trees ranked by colour – from golden yellow aspens to deep green pines – gave way to snow-covered peaks.

Durango arrived as something of a culture shock. I crossed the Animas River and turned left expecting to find a small town populated by quiet mountain folk. Instead the multi-lane highway speared its way through what appeared to be a large city, one in which everyone seemed to be rushing about, clearly with many important things to do. There were road signs everywhere: Left turn yield on flashing yellow, Right lane must turn right, Keep left, Keep right, don't do this, don't do that. I wanted to turn around and go back to the mountains. Waiting at a set of traffic lights, I saw a familiar sign. McDonald's was hardly my eatery of choice, but it seemed as good a place as any to seek refuge for a while.

I walked up to the counter and was surprised to be greeted by a middle-aged woman.

"Welcome to McDonald's, sir, what can I get you on this fine, sunny afternoon?"

Receiving such a warm and friendly greeting in a fast-food joint never ceased to catch me off guard. I ordered something at random from the menu board above her and began rifling through my pockets for cash.

"I'm afraid that'll be about thirty seconds, sir, would that be alright?" she apologised.

There was no-one else waiting to be served and I certainly had nothing better to do for the next half minute.

"Of course, I'm in no rush," I replied.

"I do apologise, sir. Perhaps you would like to take a seat and I'll bring it over to you when it's ready?"

"No, it's OK, I'll just wait here for it, saves you the trouble."

She looked at me for a few seconds, speechless. Clearly, time was a precious commodity to people in Durango. Before she could think of a response, a bell rang somewhere behind her and a disembodied hand delivered my burger. After assembling my order on a tray, she passed it to me complete with another apology.

"I hope you enjoy your meal, sir. Again, I'm very sorry for the wait."

I was mesmerised by this 'rockberg' bobbing about in the asphalt.

Concerned that she might now feel compelled to commit *seppuku* in the employee lounge for having caused a delay to my busy day of doing nothing, I retreated to a quiet table by the window.

I leafed through some of the information I'd printed off about the San Juan Skyway as I demolished my burger. I'd read that the famous Durango-Silverton narrow gauge railway was something of a highlight, but I'd not noticed any signs for it on the way in to town. You'd think a dirty great steam train would be difficult to hide anywhere, even in a metropolis like Durango. As I sat there contemplating asking the staff where the train departed from, a loud whistle pierced the air and I nearly choked on a French fry. I looked around, trying to establish where the noise had come from.

'That,' I thought to myself, 'sounded like a steam train.'

Just as that thought formed in my mind a deep rumbling filled the restaurant and an enormous black steam train passed right by the window, not five feet from where I was sitting.

'I guess that answers that question.'

Having missed seeing the train here, I picked up Highway 550 and headed along the skyway towards Silverton. By the time I reached Coal Bank Pass an hour later, I'd climbed from Durango's fairly modest

Many historical events are remembered on the skyway, such as here on the site of the Lime Creek Burn of 1879.

6,500ft to 10,660ft above sea level. It used to be only mountaineers that achieved these heights. I'd just driven here.

I made use of the remarkably clean roadside pit toilet, one that could most definitely be described as 'a loo with a view.' Engineer Mountain towered away behind me, while from the viewpoint above the trees could be seen Snowdon Peak and the three Twilight Peaks, all around 13,000ft at their summit.

Progress was slow. Not because there was anything wrong with the road; it was more that I couldn't bear to drive more than a few hundred yards without stopping to take yet more photos. In fact, from here I barely made it into second gear before pulling off the road again to photograph the unnecessarily beautiful surroundings.

Somehow I managed to string six corners together before stopping yet again, tempted this time by a fifty foot tall clump of rock that sprang out of the ground right at the tarmac's edge. Its many sedimentary layers, canted over at seventy degrees, created the impression of a rocky iceberg bobbing about in the asphalt. Its summit was crowned with aspen trees, their golden yellow leaves fluttering in the mountain breeze.

Opposite this 'rockberg' a sign had been erected, marking the site of the Lime Creek Burn of 1879. Early settlers often started wildfires to clear forested areas to make it easier to scout for mineralisation in the naked rocks, and in the case of Lime Creek the fires torched an area of some 26,000 acres. The fires were often falsely blamed on the native Utes, making it easier for them to be forced from the area thereby allowing the whites to move in. Luckily for today's visitors, a reforestation programme of seeding and replanting began in 1911 and continues to this day.

From here, I managed another ten corners before being drawn in by a rest area at Molas Pass and its views out into the Weminuche Wilderness. Named after the Weminuche Indians, it is home to three of the state's 'fourteeners' as well as several smaller but equally impressive ranges. At nearly half a million acres it's the largest wilderness area in Colorado but is technically split in two by the route of the Animas River and the Durango-Silverton railroad.

The road clung to the mountainside as it began its descent towards Silverton. The sweeping corners often lacked a guardrail, and it was difficult at times to not become distracted by the views below. As I rounded the last few bends, all of Silverton could be seen lain out before me on the valley floor.

Although earlier settlers had tried their luck, Silverton's history began in 1873 with the Brunot Treaty that allowed prospectors to tap into rich silver and gold deposits discovered in the area. Mining companies advertised in foreign newspapers, promising riches and opportunity for all, and the population swelled once the railroad reached the town in 1882. The Grand Hotel enjoyed its opening ceremony the following year, and although rebranded the Grand Imperial, it's still there today.

Mining proved to be a long-lived yet dangerous business. Cave-ins and explosions were common, but in 1978 Lake Emma collapsed into a shaft, flooded through the tunnels and eventually shot out of a portal near Cement Creek with sufficient force to topple a 20-ton locomotive.

One of several original era steam locomotives that power the Durango-Silverton narrow gauge railroad.

Even after mines were decommissioned there remained a danger. In 2015, three million gallons of water, laden with toxic elements such as cadmium, lead and arsenic, spewed out into the Animas River turning it bright orange after EPA contractors accidentally breached a plugged shaft during remedial work.

Today, most visitors come for the Durango-Silverton railroad. It has the unusual distinction of having run steam locomotives continuously since its inception, and features 1880s rolling stock with 1920s-era steam locomotives, many of which are original to the line. It's a full day out in its own right, the 45-mile route taking a rather leisurely 3½ hours to wend its way through the Animas Canyon.

From Silverton, Highway 550 takes on the more seductive title of the Million Dollar Highway, although no-one is exactly sure why. Some say it's because it cost a million dollars a mile to build, while others suggest the rock and soil excavated during its construction contained a million dollars in gold ore. Either way, it owes its origins to Colorado entrepreneur Otto Mears who built the route in 1883 as a toll road between Ouray and Ironton. It was eventually rebuilt at great expense as part of the federal highway system, re-opening in 1924.

Of course, its name could just come from the jaw-dropping views, although vertigo sufferers might struggle with the tight corners, sheer drop-offs and missing guardrails as it passes through Uncompahgre Gorge. At times, its sinuous switchbacks felt more like a racetrack, one where the penalty for getting a corner wrong is to be flung off the mountainside. I thought of the old man I'd met in Mesa Verde – it would be a brave driver who tackled this section of the route in a long vehicle like a Winnebago.

At Ridgeway the skyway leaves the 550 and takes Highway 62 west, where it begins its gentle but seemingly endless climb across the Dallas Divide (no, not that Dallas). The Divide forms a saddle between the San Juan Mountains and the thoroughly unpronounceable Uncompahgre Plateau, and is perhaps one of the most photogenic stretches of the return loop, particularly in autumn as the blue sky and snowy mountains form the perfect backdrop to acres of golden aspens. Although the gradient won't trouble any modern car, when the Rio Grande railroad used to run this way, its relentlessness required the use of extra locomotives.

No-one could ever tire of driving these roads.

The Divide eventually leads to one of the quieter stretches of the route, and when I paused by the roadside at Leopard Creek for a few minutes, not a single car passed me. It was a timely tranquil moment, with just the gentle rustling of the trees and the serene rushing of the river to occupy the silence.

I skipped the spur into the ski resort of Telluride and continued on to Rico, a small town that looked for all the world like a film set abandoned after a John Wayne western. I stopped for gas. Or at least tried to.

Gas pumps work differently in America. In the UK, there's a nozzle for each fuel whereas in the US there's just one, with the desired grade selected from a series of buttons. In America, pre-payment seems to be the norm, while in England you can merrily fill your tank and pay afterwards – a somewhat ironic situation when you consider petrol is almost four times more expensive back home. And just to confuse things, in America green nozzles are often diesel, while black ones are petrol, the reverse of that in the UK.

In Rico, I learnt something new about petrol pumps, and apparently also violated some unwritten rule about gas station etiquette. A woman was filling her car from one of the two pumps, but had parked in such a way as to make it impossible to squeeze past her to use the other pump. I was forced to sit behind her while she refuelled, and she spent much of her time shaking her head at me as if my mere presence offended her. Yes, I would have liked very much not to have to wait for her, but as she'd chosen to block the entire gas station I had no idea what she expected me to do. Perhaps American cars have a button that allows them to leapfrog the inconsiderate, but I must have missed that page in the handbook.

When she'd finally finished I drove up to the pump, pre-paid at the kiosk, slid the nozzle into the filler neck, and squeezed the trigger. Nothing happened. It was a single-grade pump, with no buttons to push or levers to pull. The guy had my money. This should have just worked. I went inside and prepared myself to play the part of the ignorant travelling Brit.

The beautiful yet endlessly distracting Dallas Divide.

"Hey, what am I doing wrong? The pump isn't working."

The guy behind the counter looked up from his books. He appeared to be the archetypal teenager earning minimum wage in a gas station to fund his college education. The books he was studying from looked old, and spread out amongst them were loose sheets of paper covered with complex-looking diagrams and formulas. He looked at me for a few seconds while his brain made the switch from calculus student to gas station attendant, and then glanced across at the pump I was parked at.

"Have you lifted the lever?" he asked.

"Which lever is that?" I made a conscious effort to pronounce it 'leh-ver' rather than confuse him with the British 'lee-ver.'

"The big black one... on the front," he said, flapping his hands around in an attempt to illustrate his explanation. "The one the thing fits into."

I wasn't sure what 'thing' related to in this conversation, but headed back outside anyway to look for a black 'leh-ver.' The only black part

I could see was the huge cradle the nozzle fitted into. It didn't seem logical to lift up such a large contraption just to turn the pump on, nor one that seemed so structural, but given I was going literally nowhere otherwise, I tried it anyway. Of course, it worked. When I went back inside to collect my change, I apologised for apparently being so inept.

"Don't worry about it," the teenager replied without looking up. "Happens all the time."

Darkness had long obscured the mountains and as I arrived in the small town of Dolores, my time on the San Juan Skyway was officially over. To this day it remains the most visually arresting journey I've ever taken, and it's easy to see how it is consistently ranked as one of America's most scenic byways.

Now, though, my thoughts turned to sleep. I could easily have checked in to any one of a number of motels in the area, but having spent much of the previous week driving 700 miles in a day, my appreciation of distance had been somewhat recalibrated. I punched 'Moab' into my satnav and when it suggested I could be in a familiar bed two hours later, the decision was made. Of course, had I known what the Super 8 staff had done, I would have made a different choice.

As is the way with satnav, two hours quickly became three, and when I finally pulled in to Moab at 2am I was about ready to collapse on the nearest park bench.

With my mind half asleep amid dreams of soft, clean bedding, I inserted my key card and tried the handle. It was locked. I took out the card and tried again. It was still locked.

Suddenly, I was wide awake. I checked the room number on the door; this was definitely my room. Expecting a simple matter of a temperamental key card, I trudged down to reception to find the night manager.

"Hi, yes, my key card doesn't seem to work," I explained to her.

"What room are you in?"

"121."

"And your name?"

"Kefford."

There was a concerning pause.

"That's not your room, sir."

"Pretty sure it is, I've been in it for a week."

She tapped away at her computer for a while, then looked up.

"You checked out this morning."

"No I didn't."

"Yes, you did."

"No, I really didn't. I'm booked to stay for another five days!"

She tapped away at her computer again. When it gave her an answer she clearly didn't like, she picked up the phone and dialled a number. She explained the predicament to whoever answered her call at 2am, whilst talking about me as if I wasn't there.

"He says he didn't check out, but the computer says different," I heard her say. I could only hear one side of the conversation, but it was obvious what had happened.

"But I can't, there's someone in there now... Well, we thought he'd gone... No, but... Yeah, but where? We can't, we're full... I don't know... That's what it says... Well, Jameson hasn't arrived yet, but... OK, but... And what do I do if he arrives?.. You're sure... Well, I suppose so."

She put the phone down and began interrogating her computer again. I'd like to meet whoever builds these all-knowing hotel computer systems and shake them warmly by the throat.

"We have a room that's booked for someone else but they haven't arrived yet, we're going to put you in there for now," she said, conveniently glossing over the fact she'd let out my room while I was still staying in it.

"Fine," I said.

Avoiding eye contact, she slid a new key card across the counter towards me, and I trudged off towards to my new room.

If that was you staying in the Moab Super 8 and you were woken by someone trying to get into your room at 2am – I'm sorry, that was me.

CHAPTER TEN

Bryce Canyon

037162

I WAS TEMPTED TO CALL out "I'll be back" *Terminator*-style as
I walked through reception in an attempt to stop the motel staff
putting someone else in my room while I was out, but thought
better of it.

Vince was having breakfast at Denny's while contemplating what to
do next. His Cherokee had certainly had its fair share of issues on this
trip, and apparently yesterday was no different.

But first, some science.

As a car turns a corner the outside wheel has to travel further than
the inside wheel, but since both have to achieve this at the same time,
they rotate at different speeds. Obviously if both wheels were attached
to a completely solid axle shaft this would be impossible, forcing us to
spend our lives driving around in straight lines. To fix this, a clever
arrangement of gears in the middle of the axle called a differential
allows the wheels to rotate at different speeds – hence the name. Now,
this is all fine and dandy in a normal road car but in a Jeep this creates
something of a problem.

Even from the road that leads into the park, the rock pinnacles are impressive.

One of the many fundamental laws of the universe, ranking somewhere near the one about bread always falling buttered side down, is that energy always follows the path of least resistance. Imagine a cup with water draining out of two holes in the bottom; covering one of the holes with your finger doesn't cause the water to force your finger away from the cup. Instead, it simply flows out of the other hole, because that's the easiest path for the water to take. This principle applies equally to an engine's power flowing through an axle. The reason why this creates a problem is that if a wheel lifts off the ground, it becomes easier to turn than those that are still on *terra firma*, and that means the Jeep goes nowhere.

To get around this, our Jeeps are equipped with locking differentials (or 'lockers') known as ARBs. Once activated by forcing compressed air through a pressure line, the lockers force the engine's power to be sent to both wheels equally, thus preventing the somewhat embarrassing situation of having one wheel in the air and a Jeep that can't move.

Unfortunately for Vince, his ARBs decided they would prefer to spend their time blowing their fuses, and this had forced him to spend yet another day troubleshooting electrical gremlins rather than enjoying his time in Moab.

There was little I could do to help; it was better to leave him to calmly and methodically work his way through the wiring until he found the root cause. In the meantime, I elected to resume my tour of America's national parks with a trip to Bryce Canyon.

Despite the name it's not really a canyon at all. Bryce lies at the edge of the Paunsaugunt Plateau as it descends the Grand Staircase towards to the Grand Canyon (which really is a canyon) and is home to the largest concentration of hoodoos – vividly coloured columns of rock formed by frost and stream erosion – anywhere on Earth. The hoodoos can be up to 200 feet high, and are frequently arranged in giant amphitheatres as much as three miles wide and 800 feet deep.

Archaeological surveys show that people have lived in the area for at least 10,000 years, and for some native Americans the hoodoos were believed to be Legend People that Coyote had mischievously turned to stone.

More modern pioneers didn't arrive until 1874 when the Church of Latter-day Saints sent Scottish immigrant Ebenezer Bryce and his wife Mary to settle in the area. He chose to establish his family below what is now Bryce Amphitheatre, the largest collection of hoodoos in

If ever a place was worthy of the name Inspiration Point, it was here at Bryce Canyon.

the park. He built log cabins, a road, and even a canal to irrigate his crops and water his animals, but he reputedly described his homestead as "a hell of a place to lose a cow." His efforts meant that others soon started to call the area 'Bryce's canyon' and when the national park was created in 1928, Ebenezer's name became immortalised.

The jaw-dropping scenery begins long before you enter the park. As the main road from the interstate passes through Red Canyon, precarious red and orange sedimentary columns peer out from behind the trees. The road even passes through the rock where two giant archways have been cut into it, while a series of hiking and biking trails peel off into the Kodachrome wilderness beyond.

As with most national parks, Bryce offers an 18-mile scenic drive that takes in many of the canyon's highlights. I'd learnt at Mesa Verde that it pays to venture a little off-piste at times and having followed an unsigned spur road I arrived at what looked like a small hotel. I was in two minds as to what to do. There was nothing to suggest I shouldn't be here, but the car park looked private and there were no other visitors around. I decided to risk it. I parked in one of the few remaining spaces and followed a discreet footpath that disappeared through the trees, unsure if it would lead towards trouble or triumph. As the trees cleared, it became obvious it was the latter. I'd found myself at Sunrise Point, staring out across Bryce Amphitheatre, littered with rocky pinnacles of red, orange and white rainbows. Some stood alone, defiantly, like a terracotta army stretching off into the distance, while others huddled together as if seeking shelter from the relentless erosion of the elements.

There was no guardrail to isolate me from the landscape, and somewhere before me in this alien terrain lay the spot a pioneering Ebenezer had chosen to call home. Hundreds of feet below I could make out narrow trails as they picked their way along the tops of peaks and dunes, while tiny visitors followed their erratic routes like mesmerised ants, stopping occasionally to take photos that could only fail to capture the humbling scale of the surroundings.

I followed the Rim Trail towards the matching Sunset Point. There, impossibly grizzled and twisted trees were perched on the very edge, their roots exposed as the soil they clung to powdered away into the colourful abyss below.

The sun pierced the clouds and threw spiky shadows out into the canyon, while taller rock formations were picked out by the warm afternoon light as if being highlighted during a presentation.

As I stood looking out across Ponderosa Canyon, a helicopter edged its way towards the plateau. Despite the chopper being 1,000ft above the canyon floor and the pilot's altimeter presumably reading 9,000ft, he and I were almost at eye level to each other. I have to admit I felt rather envious of what was probably a fantastic way to take in the best Bryce Canyon had to offer.

From Rainbow Point at the end of the scenic drive, the entirety of the park can be seen from the elevated viewpoint. The timescales might be immense, but it seemed strange to think that the very process that had created Bryce is also actively destroying it. Geologists calculate that the canyon is eroding at the rate of two to four feet every century and that within the next three million years Bryce Canyon will have disappeared altogether.

That might seem like an impossibly long time to us, but as I drove out of the park and back on to the main road, I felt privileged to have glimpsed something that, as far as the planet is concerned, will exist only for the blink of an eye.

CHAPTER ELEVEN

Capitol Reef

04025?

H IGHWAY 24 TOWARDS CAPITOL REEF is a wondrous thing. Flanked by rock cliffs as it leaves the interstate, it soon passes through an orange Martian desert with tarmac that barely deviates from arrow-straight for more than 30 miles. At Hanksville, it picks up the course of the Fremont River, either following at a respectful distance or dropping into a canyon carved out by the water over millennia. A geologist would probably take days to drive this road; around every corner, a new rock type, formation or geological feature would force them to stop to enjoy a closer inspection. To the rest of us, the road provides an ever-changing landscape of cliffs and cut-outs, plateaus and strata, all in a kaleidoscope of colours. Much of this comes right up to the roadside, while beyond, the horizon is dominated by huge structures that run for miles across the landscape like a giant perimeter wall.

The national park service, as ever, knows how to make these vast geological features accessible. Small parking lots, rest areas, and 'orientation pull-outs' (a convenient car park with pit toilets and

Petroglyphs by the roadside on the way to Capitol Reef. No-one is sure of their meaning, but they may be as much as 2,000 years old.

information boards) are frequent, while even the most remote point of interest has a laminated panel to offer some form of explanation.

I stopped at one, and was rewarded with a series of petroglyphs carved into the smooth rock perhaps more than a thousand years ago by ancestors of the Hopi and Paiute tribes. They were successful farmers, hunters, potters and rock masons, and had quickly learnt to store food in stone granaries to withstand the harsher seasons. Although little evidence exists of their habitation after 1300, these carved depictions of trapezoid-shaped people with their big-horn sheep serve as a permanent reminder of their lifestyle and culture.

Capitol Reef exists primarily to showcase the Waterpocket Fold, the longest exposed monocline in America, running for nearly 100 miles north to south like a giant spine burst through the Earth's crust. Formed by tectonic forces 35 to 75 million years ago, the west side lifted up more than 7,000 feet while the east side flattened out, exposing the nineteen or so sedimentary layers that would otherwise be completely invisible to us. As a result, a 15 mile car ride on Highway 24 allows visitors to travel through 280 million years of geological history, all without needing to resort to a plutonium-powered DeLorean.

The scale of the fold is difficult to comprehend. Clouds rolling in from my left appeared to be stopped in their tracks as they reached the fold, held back by the towering rock as it reached up into the sky. As their white cotton-wool forms gathered on one side, all they could do was cast their ominous shadows over the reef as if in a final act of defiance. Try as they might, they could go no further.

The forces that have shaped Capitol Reef since are clearly still at work today. The Scenic Drive often descends steeply into a concrete-bottomed wash-out, while frequent signs make it clear not to enter the area if a rain storm is even vaguely likely. Flash floods arrive with little or no warning, and it can be hours or even days before it's possible to drive out of the canyons.

Despite the risks, Capitol Gorge was originally the only way for early settlers to cross the reef. In 1884 Mormon pioneers spent eight days clearing the natural gorge of rocks and other debris, a process that had to be repeated after every flash flood. Early travellers often recorded their relief at a successful passage through the gorge by inscribing their names on the canyon walls, now known as Pioneer

As geological features go, the reef is pretty big. Large enough to stop weather, in fact.

Register. Remarkably, the gorge remained a public road until Highway 24 was completed in 1962.

It took a special type of person to live here. The first permanent settlement was established in 1880 in an area now known as Fruita, but no more than ten families ever lived here at a time. Life would have been hard with many challenges, not the least of which was the need to be entirely self-sufficient.

A preserved homestead offers a glimpse of how things would have been. Built in 1908, its longest inhabitants were the Gifford family who occupied the home from 1928 until 1969. They were adept farmers with cows, pigs and sheep but also grew crops such as potatoes, corn, and peas. The area had long been associated with fruit production – perhaps the reason for the name – and today its orchards are honoured by the sale of locally-produced fruit jams and pies from inside the homestead.

I'm sure life here would have been demanding – electricity didn't arrive until 1948, for example – but I couldn't help but find the bucolic idyll offered by this calm oasis desperately appealing, despite the foreboding surroundings.

The Gifford Homestead, and the family's home until 1969.

CHAPTER TWELVE

Lockhart Basin

04155

I FOUND MYSELF TORN. TORN between two road-trips. On the one hand, I had the chance to fulfil a long-held ambition to visit as many of America's national parks as possible. But on the other, Vince and I had gone to the rather extreme trouble of shipping our Jeeps all the way to the US, and that demanded that we use them properly.

There was little I could do to square this particular circle; I couldn't do two road-trips at the same time. I had to make peace with the fact that while Zion, Death Valley, Grand Canyon and even the mighty Yellowstone all fell within driving distance of Moab, there was just no way I could see them all.

I promised myself I'd find a way to squeeze in one more park before we had to leave. In the meantime, we headed back into the red Martian dust of Moab.

~

Ledges and drop-offs are the order of the day on Lockhart Basin.

I'd never seen blue rocks before. Red, yes. In fact in Moab you're perpetually surrounded by them, together with various shades of orange, white, and almost everything in between. But blue? That was a new one on me. Although I should probably mention at this point that I'm technically colour-blind, so who knows what colour they really were.

We were on our way to tackle Lockhart Basin, one of the longest trails in Moab at roughly 37 miles and rated moderately difficult, thanks largely to the many off-camber ledges and boulder-strewn wash-outs that need to be negotiated on the way to the basin itself.

There's enough here to catch out the unwary. Many of the canyon climbs are narrow, made narrower by boulders the size of houses that jut out into the trail's path. The ascents can be steep and are littered with small, loose rocks that spin under the Jeep's tyres, flinging them down the trail and forcing you off-line.

Choosing the best line is crucial, but it's a line that changes every season as run-off water erodes the surface and deposits the rocky debris in a new location after every rainfall.

Thirty seven miles might not sound like much, but it'll take the average Jeeper a good six hours to complete the trail. It's started to become popular with mountain bikers, too, although I was surprised to discover they prefer to ride it in reverse which means the obstacles get progressively harder the further they venture along the trail. They at least seem to have the good sense to bring a tent and make a couple of days of it, with the added bonus of being the best way to experience the sheer desolation.

We switched off the Jeeps' engines and stood quietly for a few minutes; not a single sound could be heard, not even the wind. After a while I thought I could hear an approaching motorbike, but couldn't decide at first whether it was just my imagination or perhaps the deafening sound of my heartbeat pounding in my ears. With that, a motor-cross rider power-slid through the rock dust and around the corner, perhaps equally surprised to come across a pair of Jeeps as we were to see him in this isolated landscape. We waved our mutual respect to each other and he roared off up the trail.

There are several unwritten rules in Moab, but the one we were keen to follow stipulates that 4x4 drivers should offer water to any hikers or bikers they encounter on the trail. The average mountain biker will need to consume several gallons while out in Utah's hot, dry air, and it's not always practical to carry such a large amount. A four-wheeled packhorse like a Jeep, meanwhile, can carry comparatively unlimited water supplies without breaking a sweat, and we made sure the few people we met on the trail were sufficiently well watered. Most wore CamelBaks – a water-filled bladder with a drinking tube carried on the back like a rucksack – as did we, although at least a couple were grateful of the chance to top up.

After six bumpy and dusty hours on the trail, we dropped back onto the main road and steered in the direction of Moab. But we had one stop to make on the way.

Newspaper Rock sits just off State Road 211 and is perhaps the largest and most accessible petroglyph panel in Utah. The 200 square foot slab of sandstone has been covered with more than 650 symbols etched into the black manganese-iron coating – often called 'desert varnish' – that's common to these red-rock cliffs. Although no-one knows for sure the purpose of the various human, animal and other abstract symbols, they are believed to represent nearly 2,000 years of early human history spanning the Basketmaker, Fremont, ancestral Puebloan, Navajo, and even Anglo cultures that settled in the area. In Navajo, the rock is called *Tse' Hone* which translates as 'rock that tells a story' and from there it's a small jump to the more modern 'Newspaper Rock.'

Today we might prefer to read about the day's events on our smartphones, but this giant lump of sandstone will still be here long after your iPhone has been consigned to landfill.

Newspaper Rock will probably still be here long after we are gone.

CHAPTER THIRTEEN

Steel Bender

04189♫

C AMELBAKS WERE FILLED, TYRES AIRED down, and fuel
tanks topped off. We were ready.
"This is why we shipped the Jeeps all the way here," said
Vince, as we began our descent into Mill Creek through a series of
tight switchbacks.

Steel Bender changes with the seasons but generally isn't a trail for
the feint-hearted. Nor is it one you should tackle in a standard vehicle;
lockers, a respectable suspension lift and 33-inch tyres or bigger are
considered a bare minimum. As is a generous lump of off-roading
experience and a healthy respect for the terrain.

Having brought our own Jeeps with us we had the luxury of knowing
that, ultimately, we were only responsible to ourselves and not some
waiver-brandishing rental company should anything go wrong. In
fact, most Jeep rental outfits have banned their vehicles from trails like
Steel Bender due to the high likelihood of sustaining damage.

The trail starts seductively easily. Sandy tracks wind their way
through the trees at the base of the canyon, crossing the creek several

Lining the Wrangler up prior to a steep rocky descent.

times, before climbing a series of rocky shelves and ledges that hint at what's to come.

For many this offers a good chance to practice a technique we'd already used on Fins 'n' Things, although it wasn't until Steel Bender that we learnt it was officially known as the 'Moab bump' technique. This involves slowly rolling the front tyres up and over an obstacle and, just as the rear tyres are two or three feet from the ledge, blipping the throttle to create enough momentum to carry them over. Not enough power or applying it too late results in little more than the rear tyres spinning against the ledge and your trail buddies laughing at you for being a 'newbie.' Too much power and there's a very real chance of breaking something important like a driveshaft as the Jeep lurches against the ledge.

There's an old joke in Moab that says "if you don't like the weather, just wait half an hour." Before we left the motel we'd heard the local weather reports talk of rain but dismissed it as hubris. No sooner had we started our ascent than the heavens opened. Rain fell out of the sky at a rate I'd never experienced before, the Jeep's wipers utterly failing to make any headway against the deluge landing on the windscreen. The trail disappeared beneath a river that formed out of nowhere, forcing us to stop and wait. To continue would have been foolhardy – boulders and ledges vanished as they became submerged, making it impossible to choose a line through an obstacle.

And yet, just as the old joke said, half an hour later the rain stopped abruptly and the blue sky returned. Almost as quickly as it had appeared, the river we were parked in dissipated and the trail revealed itself. Within another few minutes, the surrounding slickrock was bone dry, leaving no trace of the monsoon we'd just experienced. It was almost a figment of our imagination.

Steel Bender is known for three obstacles in particular. The first, nicknamed The Wall, looks far scarier through the windscreen than it is in reality. A steep scramble up a six-foot high slickrock fin, it's easily achievable by sticking to an arrow-straight line and deploying the Moab bump technique. Less confident drivers, or those that perhaps haven't had their morning caffeine fix yet, will be glad to find there is a bypass route.

The second, known as The Fall, is a rocky descent that has caught out many an experienced driver. The trail turns sharply left here as it drops off an 8ft ledge. Get it wrong and there's a very real chance of performing a gymnastic nose-stand, followed by rolling over off the sheer cliff edge and into the canyon below. The previous day a Wrangler had suffered that exact fate, and as we jumped out of the Jeeps to assess our strategy, its upended carcass was a timely reminder that this can easily all go very wrong.

Having a Jeep with a short rear overhang makes it less likely to snag the bumper as the rear wheels drop down, although years of rock-stacking – piling small rocks at the base of an obstacle to lessen the gradient – has made it less likely to buckle a Wrangler's tailgate if the spare tyre clips the drop-off.

That doesn't make it less likely to sustain damage elsewhere, however, and as our group filtered its way through The Fall, we noticed small drops of oil left behind on the dry slickrock. Clearing them up

A punctured rear diff cover wasn't going to stop us for long.

and a quick scout through the convoy revealed one of our group had punctured their rear differential cover.

Fixing vehicles on the trail is just another part of the experience. Far from getting annoyed at the hold-up caused by someone's misfortune, a trail fix is more of an opportunity to prove the camaraderie that exists between fellow four-wheelers. While the unlucky victim broke out his tools and crawled under his Jeep, others in the group fetched whatever they could to make the job easier: a container to drain the axle oil into, a tube of ATV sealant, fresh gear oil, a torque wrench. Many hands make light work, so the proverb tells us, and in next to no time the issue was resolved and we were back on our way.

Just in time to tackle the third and most notorious obstacle of the trail – Dragon's Tail. Technically it's more of a series, a mile-long run of rocky ledges and shelves culminating with Dragon's Head. Each has a bypass to one side, but where's the fun in that? Many of the ledges are both huge and off-camber, and it's here that the relationship between driver and spotter is really tested.

At Witches Step the ledges form a momentum-sapping staircase that leads to two large shelves at the summit, while the spacing between them tends to favour the longer wheelbase of a Cherokee over the shorter Wrangler. We were both grateful for the ground clearance advantage our 35-inch tyres gave us over others in the group. What we perhaps hadn't anticipated was quite how much our new suspension would take some getting used to. On side-slopes and off-camber drop-offs, the Jeeps would tip alarmingly as their weight transferred and the suspension unloaded on one side. It didn't cause a problem as such, but was definitely something to be aware of.

The trail continued to deliver a mixture of sandy switchbacks and rocky ledges until it dropped again into Mill Creek. Mirroring the day's start, our convoy squeezed its way through the trees, crossed the river, and clambered up the steep bank on the other side.

Vince tackling the final ledge on Witches Step.

From here, the trail reverted to an easy gravel road through Kens Lake campground and on to the tarmac road beyond.

Steel Bender might be only 15 miles or so in length, but it had taken our group the better part of seven hours. I felt sure I could speak for everyone when I said I was ready for a cold beer.

~

Our Moab-themed bingo scorecard swelled over the next few days as yet more trails were successfully ticked off.

Rose Garden Hill with its steep rocky gradients at times so strewn with boulders that it's easy to get stuck while going downhill.

Flat Iron Mesa and its nerve-racking squeeze past Easter Egg Rock just as another rock tips the Jeep over towards it, often forcing spectators to act as human ground-anchors.

Elephant Hill with its narrow slot between two sheer rock cliffs offering only millimetres to spare either side, and where a Cherokee in our group unfortunately succumbed to water ingestion as a consequence of rescuing a cyclist from a flash flood the day before.

And Strike Ravine with its boulder-field wash-outs that stand ready to unseat tyres and bend steering gear at every turn.

None of this would have been possible in a pair of rental Jeeps. And although Vince's Cherokee had experienced its fair share of teething problems, we felt lucky to be able to say that not once did we bend or break anything on a trail.

CHAPTER FOURTEEN

Canyonlands

`04276户`

T HIS WAS TO BE OUR last full day in Moab. If I was the superstitious type, I'd perhaps suggest that Utah knew we were leaving. Gone were the sapphire blue skies and golden sunshine we'd grown used to during our time here, replaced by moody clouds and the warning of an incoming storm. But I was determined to squeeze in one last national park before we hit the road to complete our coast-to-coast road-trip. Choosing not to venture too far in case the weather took a turn for the worse, I headed for Canyonlands.

We'd skirted through the park in the Jeeps several times while following a few of the off-road trails, but this was the first time through the gate, so to speak. Beyond the various canyons that give the park its name, it's perhaps most famous for being the point where the Colorado and Green Rivers merge, creating the confluence. It's an area popular with kayakers and rafters, particularly as the stretches below the confluence are peppered with powerful white-water rapids.

Much like Mesa Verde, Canyonlands retains evidence of ancestral Puebloan cultures, some of which – like the aptly-named Roadside Ruin – can be seen... well, from the roadside.

European settlers explored the area in the early 1800s but it's perhaps not until the Mormon church expanded its missionary efforts that settlement became more permanent. Ranchers built simple trails to move livestock through the terrain, with some of the pioneering families retaining their holdings here until comparatively recently.

But it wasn't just livestock that took shelter here; a certain Robert Leroy Parker, better known as Butch Cassidy, sought refuge in the especially rugged terrain of The Maze, as did many other outlaws.

Today it's mostly deer, rodents and reptiles that roam the multitude of ecosystems within the park, although bobcats and mountain lions are also known to live here. On a smaller scale, pools of water that form in the uneven sandstone surfaces quickly become home to microbes, shrimp and other creatures. They also provide a source of drinking water to many of the park's animals, just as they did to early settlers hundreds of years ago. At Pothole Point the other-worldly landscape appears littered with them.

However, as I stood there looking out across to The Needles – great spires of rock, not unlike the hoodoos I'd seen at Bryce Canyon – I could see a new concern coming over the horizon.

Is that smoke billowing towards us?

Dense black clouds were rolling towards me, and in the distance as they discharged their watery contents onto the landscape below, they took on an appearance more like rising foreboding smoke.

I'd been warned by the ranger at the park gate not to enter the low-lying areas if it looked like the rains would come. The road I'd followed had descended some distance, too, making it a place you very seriously didn't want to be anywhere near if there was even a chance of a flash flood. I looked around and, other than a pair of Japanese tourists who were engrossed in photographing every inch of Big Spring Canyon, it appeared I was by now the only visitor in this part of the park.

The sky grew darker in the moments that I stood there, and the clouds drew nearer. Increasingly I was filled with the sense that I really shouldn't be there. When the TV news covers the rescue of a hiker who'd decided the best time to climb a mountain was during a snowstorm, or when a little old lady in a Cadillac tries to drive through a mudslide to get to church, I often find myself wondering what was going through their minds in the moments just before disaster struck. Did the snowstorm creep up on them undetected? Or did sheer hubris lead to the dismissal of danger with the simple thought: 'No, I'm sure everything will be fine.' However it happens, I was beginning to feel a little like that myself.

I shouted to the Japanese tourists and, as they turned to look at me, I pointed towards the gathering storm behind them. The wind had picked up and any verbal communication between us would have been swept aside by the incoming gale, but they turned to see what I was pointing at. The sight that greeted them spoke for itself. They waved their acknowledgement and we both started back to our cars.

Had I known quite how bad the storm was going to be, I might have been a little more insistent.

CHAPTER FIFTEEN

Moab to
Mexican Hat

044022

T HE LOCAL NEWS WAS ON the TV while I packed up my belongings. It seemed strange to be leaving the Super 8. It had been my home for the last two weeks, despite an attempt at early eviction, and although it was hardly glamorous it had been a convenient springboard for so much.

The anchor-man was talking rather excitedly about the weather but I wasn't paying a great deal of attention. However, when he handed over to the weatherman the talk of flash floods made me stop what I was doing. I glanced at the TV just as the satellite forecast revealed a giant swirling cloud mass heading straight for Moab. I threw back the curtains and instead of the blue sky and desert terrain that had been my view for the last fortnight, I was greeted by a window on to a world obscured by thick fog and torrential rain.

We had hoped we could tackle a final few trails before leaving Moab, but when the weatherman mentioned localised flooding I knew our plans were going to have to change.

I dragged my belongings through a car park strewn with puddles and squeezed them in to the back of the Wrangler, before meeting Vince for breakfast at Denny's one last time.

"I hear many of the trails are closed already due to flooding," Vince remarked as he sliced into his pancakes.

"Did you see the forecast this morning? One guy was talking about it being the worst storm for a generation," I agreed.

Both our Jeeps were equipped with snorkels, a raised air intake that allows the engine to continue breathing even when driving through deep water, but that doesn't make them immune to the laws of physics. If fast-moving water can drag huge boulders across a road, a Jeep can be easily tossed about.

"What do you want to do, then?" I asked Vince, seeking a consensus. I was reluctant to call a halt to our plans, but it would be tough to explain how we survived two weeks in Moab without incident only to trash the Jeeps on the last day.

"We've done plenty of trails while we've been here, all without damage. We should quit while we're ahead. Plus if we leave now we might be able to get ahead of the storm." The logic of it was undeniable. Much as we'd love to stay here forever, the reality was that we had to leave sometime.

Pulling out of the Super 8 parking lot and back on to the 191, I took up my old position behind Vince's Cherokee. There was something strange about being here again. It was familiar, yes, like returning to work after a two week vacation, but so much had happened in the time since that I couldn't shake the feeling I'd been somehow altered by it. Today's itinerary, for example, called for us to drive roughly 130 miles; having spent so much of the last few weeks driving anything up to 700 miles in a day, by comparison this felt like nipping out for a pint of milk.

We did appear to be doing it in something of a monsoon, though. The Wrangler's miniature wipers struggled to keep the windscreen clear, perhaps not helped by the rooster-tails of spray being thrown up into the air by the Cherokee's tyres.

For me, much of the first part of our journey should have been familiar. I'd followed this same road on my way to the San Juan Skyway, but as I peered out of the Jeep's fogged-up windows nothing looked as it did back then. The air was heavy and grey, and giant water droplets pelted the windscreen like diamonds. For the second time, it felt like we were driving through a cloud that had slipped its tether and crashed down to earth.

As we approached the small town of Bluff the road dropped into a canyon, the tarmac bounded by steep cliffs that rose up on both sides. Bluff is perhaps most famous for its Twin Rocks Trading Post, a ranch-style souvenir shop and café that sits right below two towering sandstone pillars, said to be a symbol of the Hero Twins of Navajo legend. The twins, named *Nayénzgan* (Slayer of Monsters) and *Tobadzîschíni* (Child of Water), were born of a relationship between Changing Woman and the Sun, and together they are said to have rid the Earth of monsters that had prayed upon their people, earning them a place in mythology.

The road climbed out of the canyon and through a channel cut across a rocky backbone. The clouds began to lift and we left the rain behind. By the time we crossed into the Navajo Reservation at Mexican Hat, the sun was beginning to burn through the fringes of cloud cover, offering glimpses of the clear blue sky beyond.

Mexican Hat often finds itself on a list of places with unusual names. It should come as no surprise, then, that its name comes from a rock that's shaped a bit like a sombrero. With a population of just 31, it's probably also no surprise that there isn't much else to shout about, and it boasts just two places to stay: Mexican Hat Lodge, which I was disappointed to discover isn't shaped like a hat, and the San Juan Inn, perched on the banks of the river of the same name and our home for the evening.

It was very different to the motels we'd stayed in before. We'd somehow been lucky enough to book what amounted to a small apartment, complete with a kitchen and living room. Our accommodation formed the second floor above the reception block

Our motel apartment was surrounded by wooden decking that merged into the red rock cliffs behind.

and was surrounded on all sides by wooden decking. The back of the building butted up against huge red cliffs that formed part of the Goosenecks State Park, and where the rock jutted out the decking had been artfully cut around it, blurring the line between the two. On the opposite side of the building, the decking formed a balcony that looked out over the parking lot, across to the restaurant and bar, and to the San Juan River beyond.

In stark contrast to our usual habit of pulling into a motel at well past midnight and tired beyond all comprehension, we had arrived at the San Juan Inn at a thoroughly respectable time in the late afternoon. Out of nowhere, Vince produced a couple of bottles of beer; considering we were still in Utah with its completely unfathomable alcohol laws, I had no idea where he got them from. Nor, frankly, did I care, and we sat on the balcony drinking our beers, presumably breaking several laws in the process, as the evening sun began to edge closer to the horizon.

I broke out the laptop and scrolled through a few local news sites. As it turned out, our decision to leave Moab to get ahead of the storm had been a good one. Heavy rain had swept through much of Utah throughout the day, triggering flash floods, breaching river banks, and causing power outages and rock slides. Hanksville – that I'd driven through just three days before on my way to Capitol Reef – was under three feet of water, while Highway 24 that I'd so admired had been clean washed away by the storm waters. The Fremont River that runs through the town had swelled from a relatively tranquil flow rate of 39 cubic feet per second to a staggering 3,600, while the nearby Dirty Devil River (typically 72 ft³/s) became a veritable raging torrent at 14,000. A school bus full of children found themselves stranded for hours on what remained of the highway, with rescuers having to resort to a hovercraft to reach them. One news report quoted Hanksville's Mayor as saying: "We have water everywhere. We can just as well call Hanksville a lake. That is about what it is right now."

We'd clearly been incredibly lucky. The realisation dawned on us, as we sat on the balcony enjoying our cold beers, that had we left Moab just half an hour later, we'd have been caught up in some inescapable watery catastrophe.

Having by now spent much of the afternoon staring down at the motel's restaurant from our balcony, we thought we ought to pay it a visit. A neon Budweiser sign shone through one of the windows, indicating either the alcohol laws here were more relaxed or, perhaps more likely, they just didn't care. We found ourselves a table and sat down, at least half expecting to be told to move.

There was only one other customer in the restaurant. Perched on a stool at the bar, the old man was staring into the bottom of his glass at the token mouthful of beer that remained there. I assumed him to be a regular, which I took to mean the food was at least safe to eat, although it may simply have been that he was wise enough to avoid it.

A woman dressed in Navajo-style clothing sidled up to the table, but didn't say a word. She handed us a pair of menus and, again without saying anything, returned to the safety of the bar. The menu was much

The motel restaurant beckoned to us from our lofty balcony, until we could resist no longer.

as you'd expect – burgers, steaks, and so on – but I was mesmerised by one particular item that, try as I might, I couldn't divert my attention away from.

"What do you imagine a Navajo Bean Pizza is?" I asked Vince, somewhat rhetorically.

"Could be anything. Is it a Navajo pizza or is it a regular pizza with Navajo beans on?" he wondered out loud.

What I did know was that I was all burgered out, and if I ate another pancake there was a very real danger I would start to look like one.

"I'm going to have to try it, there's just nothing else for it," I relented, looking over at the woman behind the bar in an attempt to catch her eye. Finally she looked up from what she was reading, and casually sauntered across to our table.

"I'll try the Navajo Bean Pizza, please," I said proudly.

She stared at me for a while, with an expression I couldn't quite place. Perhaps it was the surprise of someone being stupid enough to order the Navajo Bean Pizza.

"And a coffee, please," I added, more in an attempt to stir her into action than anything else.

Eventually she diverted her gaze to her notepad, raised her eyebrows almost imperceptibly, and wrote down my order. Looking across to Vince, she took down his far safer and more conventional choice and then retreated to the kitchen, again without speaking a word.

"If whatever this pizza is should kill me," I joked to Vince once she was out of earshot, "I just want to say... it's been a blast."

She returned a few minutes later with two mugs and a glass jug of coffee which she proceeded to pour, again without recourse to the English language.

"Thank-you," we both said as she retired to the kitchen.

She was back some time later with our food, setting it down on the table before us without uttering a syllable. As it turns out a Navajo Bean Pizza isn't really a pizza at all. It's perhaps more of a flan, and on to this particular one had been emptied what appeared to be a tin of baked beans that was struggling to be corralled by the pastry rim. Despite its rather poverty-stricken looks it actually tasted fine. However, it was undoubtedly the most filling dish ever devised by mankind and I struggled to eat more than a quarter before having to admit defeat. I felt hopelessly guilty at the quantity of food left on my plate when the woman returned to clear them away.

Thankfully, she didn't say anything about it.

CHAPTER SIXTEEN

Monument Valley to Las Vegas

04849⏎

WE EACH HAD A LIST of things we wanted to achieve during this trip. During the prep nine months ago, when we'd spread a series of maps out across the living room carpet, Vince had pointed to one spot in particular with some conviction.

"Whatever happens, we need to make sure we get photos of us driving through Monument Valley," he'd demanded. "That has to be one of the most famous stretches of road anywhere in the world, and we can't ship the Jeeps all the way to the US and not get photos there," he'd said, not unreasonably.

As it happens, Monument Valley sits less than ten miles from Mexican Hat, so Vince's wish was about to come true.

Many a film has been shot here, from *Easy Rider* to *Back to the Future*, but perhaps the one that became most lodged in popular culture is *Forrest Gump*. Tom Hanks' character ended his cross-country run of three years, two months, fourteen days and sixteen hours here,

with the Monument Valley buttes providing the most recognisable of backdrops. There's even a sign by the side of the road now marking Forrest Gump Point. We were lucky there were very few people around, allowing us to set up a few shots before I risked being run over by a slow-moving Winnebago.

Five minutes later we crossed into Arizona, our thirteenth state. A small sign welcomed us to 'the Grand Canyon State' while a series of ramshackle Navajo jewellery and souvenir stalls punctuated the roadside.

At Tuba City we pulled into a garage to fill up the Jeeps. Considering we had been using our British credit cards for most of the trip, we'd had remarkably little trouble paying for gas. Occasionally we had stumbled across a station that insisted on pre-payment, for which we'd used cash, but for most of the time our flexible friends had done us proud. I guess that only made it inevitable that at some point our luck would run out.

Many petrol pumps in America have a slot and a keypad that allow you to pay without leaving the forecourt, and the pump Vince and I were leaning against in Tuba City was no different. What was different, however, was that this one was refusing to recognise Vince's credit card. Or mine, for that matter.

We'd tried various tactics – inserting the card slowly, inserting it quickly, blowing on it first, rubbing it, even standing on one leg and singing a little song like some kind of rain dance. None of this had worked, and by now having two British-registered Jeeps with weird number plates blocking off two pumps in a busy gas station was beginning to attract a level of attraction we felt we could do without.

Admitting defeat, we wandered into the gas station and spoke to the cashier.

"What the hell kind of bank is Abbey National?" he asked, perhaps not unreasonably.

"It's a British bank, we're from England. But it's still a Visa card so it should work fine."

The cashier turned the card over in his hands several times, although I have no idea what he was looking for. He glanced out across the forecourt at the two Jeeps, the line of cars waiting to fill up behind us, and the two gas pumps that weren't currently earning him any money.

"Just fill 'em up and we'll do the slips by hand," he relented.

Relieved, we headed back out to the Jeeps and topped off the tanks. When we returned to the cashier, he produced a couple of carbon sales slips and one of those sliding card imprinter machines that I'd not seen in years. Rather clumsily he took payment manually, complete with the retro experience of hearing that 'kra-chunk' noise as he slid the machine across each credit card, and we were released from our involuntary detention.

"I think this might be a good time to stop for lunch," I suggested to Vince, having spied a Subway just behind the gas station. "But let's pay cash this time."

"Good idea."

Subway had become another of our 'go to' places during this trip. Most small towns seemed to have one somewhere, as did many service areas. In fact, there are nearly 25,000 in the US alone, making them bigger than McDonald's or even Starbucks. On this visit, however, there was something of a language barrier between us.

"We're doing a special today, sir. Would you like chips with that?" the lady behind the counter asked me.

This was more than a little confusing. Subway sold everything you could think of to squeeze inside a sandwich, plus a few things you hadn't, but I'd never seen chips inside a sub before. And while the vast array of stainless steel trays before me were filled with toppings such as meatballs, tuna, lettuce, olives, and the omnipresent yellow plastic cheese, chips were nowhere to be seen. Besides, wouldn't they be called fries here?

"Chips?" I asked, hoping for clarification of some kind.

"Chips, sir," she repeated, matter-of-factly.

She pointed at another counter behind me. There, arranged in neat little rows, were various multi-coloured plastic bags. I took a step closer hoping for some hint as to their contents: 'Potato Chips' one label declared.

"Ah, crisps! We call them crisps where I come from," I retorted, again sounding like some displaced Mary Poppins character. "Yes, I'll have some chips, thanks."

The lady behind the counter smirked at her crazy English customer and my apparent inability to use my own language.

Two hours later we joined the I-40 at Flagstaff. It seemed strange to be on an interstate again. I'd spent so long driving in the middle of nowhere, through deserts and mountains, that a freeway felt like an alien environment to me.

For much of its path through Arizona, the I-40 traces the route of one of the most famous roads in the world – Route 66 – from Lupton on the Arizona/New Mexico border to just before Seligman where the two diverge. I'd have loved nothing more than to peel off the highway and follow it all the way to Santa Monica, but that's a whole other road-trip. Several packs of Harleys overtook us on their way to pick up the rest of Route 66, leaving only the fumes of unburnt petrol and a growing sense of jealousy in their wake.

As we reached Seligman, we pulled off the interstate briefly to refuel. We didn't know it at the time, but the Shell garage we'd chosen happened to be the most notorious in the state for non-paying drive-offs. For the second time, we were about to pick a fight with an Arizona gas pump.

After a couple of false starts, the pump appeared to accept my credit card and 91 Premium began flowing into the Wrangler's tank. Vince, in front of me, I could see was having trouble. I left the Wrangler refuelling and went to investigate.

"What's up, Vince?" I asked.

There was swearing. Vince doesn't swear often so frustration levels were clearly high.

"It rejected my first card, and now this one's just been declined. It's ridiculous!" Vince sighed, angrily. "We've driven through thirteen states and refuelled in some seriously dodgy areas without a single

Apparently, this is Arizona's most notorious gas station for drive-offs.

problem. But here in Arizona, we have a 100% failure rate. It's just gas, it's not like I'm buying a car or something!"

"Do you want to use mine? Seems to be working at the moment," I offered, pointing back towards the Wrangler but with the fingers on my other hand crossed behind my back in case the pump changed its mind.

"I have one card left," Vince replied with finality, holding it up to glint in the sunlight as if it were the Holy Grail of personal finance.

He placed the card in the slot and hit the 91 button on the pump. There was a pause while the state of Arizona decided if we were to be allowed to continue our journey. Eventually, the pump beeped angrily and displayed a single word on its tiny screen: "BLOCKED."

This time, we both swore.

I don't think it's overstating things to say that credit cards are a matter of life and death when you're thousands of miles from home. Without them, we can't pay for fuel, food or a place to stay, and should the worst happen and one of us have an accident, they'd be critical to accessing medical care. Having a card declined or, worse, blocked can easily spell disaster. Not only that, but because we were nearing the end of our trip, we were both running low on cash.

Although ATMs are plentiful, many don't accept international cards. The ones that do are exceptionally paranoid. On almost every occasion where one of us found a machine willing to dispense dollars in to our hot little hands, after doing so it would bring down the metaphorical shutters and refuse to honour any subsequent request, with the added risk of potentially swallowing our card never to be seen again.

Vince headed in to the gas station to try to find a way of resolving this particular impasse with the cashier. He returned a few minutes later with his phone to his ear and the look of someone being subjected to particularly awful hold music.

"The bank blocked my card," he said, angling the mouthpiece away from his face. I could only hear one side of the conversation, but I knew I wouldn't have wanted to be on the other end.

"Yes, but I told you weeks ago that I'd be in America.... Why would you block this transaction and not the others?... But I've been to countless other gas stations without a problem... No... I literally cannot go anywhere until you unblock my card... No... Look, I'm standing in the middle of nowhere. There's nothing for miles around but mountains and this gas station... Yes, and the other cards, too... Because I need them... I can't go to my branch, can I, I'm five thousand miles away!... You speak to them instead."

With that, Vince marched back in to the gas station. He returned a few minutes later, shaking his head.

"Looks like I'm solvent again," he said. And with that, the pump whirred into life and twenty gallons of Shell's finest flowed into the Cherokee's fuel tank.

We were by now somewhat behind schedule. As had become customary on this trip, time was short; our itinerary called for 450 miles to Las Vegas before nightfall, and we were still only half way there. We rejoined the interstate, determined to claw back some time,

An ingenuous way to transport four tractor units - by piggyback!

although that sentiment was paused slightly when we saw... well... four trucks mating.

I'd spotted them in my rear-view mirror when they were still some distance away, but couldn't quite work out what I was seeing. At first glance, it looked like four tractor units following each other dangerously closely, but as they drew nearer I could see they had all been interlinked. The lead truck was pulling the other three, but each truck had been somehow driven partially on to the back of the one before it, leaving only the rearmost wheels on the ground. I couldn't begin to imagine how this was possible, nor could I picture the conversation when someone had first suggested it. Instead I just marvelled at their ingenuity as the conjoined trucks rumbled by.

Much as we'd wanted to stop in Kingman, a popular point on Route 66 and the location for many a cult film such as *Two-Lane Blacktop*, time as always was against us. As the signs for the Grand Canyon started to appear at the side of US-93, Vince and I had another difficult choice before us.

While the Grand Canyon regularly appears on the list of America's top tourist destinations, we'd spent the last few weeks driving in, on and through some of the wildest and most awe-inspiring canyons and mountain ranges this great country has to offer. At this point, it was difficult to see how a tourist trap like the Grand Canyon could top that. Having visited Mesa Verde, Bryce Canyon, Capitol Reef and Canyonlands I, in particular, felt more than a little 'canyoned-out.' Almost without a word, then, the last sign for the Grand Canyon came into view, and then receded in our mirrors as neither Jeep made the turn towards it.

There was somewhere we were determined not to miss, however, and we were conscious of the fact we were already beginning to lose the light.

Hoover Dam straddles the Arizona/Nevada border where it holds back Lake Mead, America's largest reservoir. Built in 1931-36, it supplies flood control, water regulation and hydroelectric power to the citizens of Arizona, Nevada and California, generating as much as 4 billion kWh each year. The dam itself is simply massive: 726 feet tall, at its base the dam is 660 feet thick, narrowing to 45 feet at the top where Highway 93 used to run until a bypass opened in 2010. Its construction required nearly 4.5 million cubic yards of concrete, 21,000 men, and cost $49 million – roughly $800 million in today's money. Amazingly, it was completed two years ahead of schedule.

Today the dam is operated by the Department of Reclamation, and they happily lay on a series of tours that descend into the bowels of the dam and the power plant below. Unless you arrive late like us, that is. In which case you'll have to make do with walking across the top and marvelling not just at the scale of the engineering, but also the Art Deco detailing. The 30ft high winged bronze figures were apparently cast in one continuous pour, while some of the impressive reliefs carry inscriptions that are surprisingly touching for a piece of civil engineering. One plaque is dedicated to the 96 men who died during the dam's construction, and carries an inscription that begins simply: "they died to make the desert bloom." The two elevator towers feature reliefs moulded in concrete. One illustrates the purpose of the dam – flood control, navigation, irrigation, water storage, and power –

while the other depicts scenes of American Indian life. With them, an inscription reads: "Since primordial times, American Indian tribes and Nations lifted their hands to the Great Spirit from these ranges and plains. We now with them in peace buildeth again a Nation."

I couldn't help but think back to the great British engineers of Victorian times, an era when even something as humble as a bridge or a water pumping station would be adorned with intricately carved forms and decorated with ornate painted scrollwork. Today this pride in our achievements seems to have been lost, perhaps a casualty of capitalism and the endless desire to maximise profit. As I stood at the edge of the dam looking down on to a structure built more than 70 years ago, I was overwhelmed by a sense of admiration. Hoover Dam is a creation of which the American people should rightly feel proud.

Vince dares to look down towards the bottom of Hoover Dam.

With the light fading we crossed the dam into Nevada – our fourteenth state and yet another time zone – and pushed on to Las Vegas.

Vegas rose out of the Mojave Desert before us as the interstate rounded a corner, a calm, flat sea of lights glinting and twinkling in the darkness. Although officially incorporated in 1911, its success owes much to the Hoover Dam. In 1931, the same year dam construction began, casino gambling was legalised by the state of Nevada. As construction workers and their families flooded into the area, they brought economic prosperity with them, helping Las Vegas to withstand the vagaries of the Great Depression. The boom continued well into the post-war years, and in 1959 the iconic 'Welcome to Fabulous Las Vegas' sign was designed by Betty Willis and placed at the southern end of the famous 'strip.' Ironically, the sign isn't actually in Las Vegas at all. Instead it lies roughly four miles to the south of the city limits, placing it in a region known as Paradise, along with all the outlandish casinos and hotels that come to mind when we think of the city.

Whatever the place was called, we were having trouble navigating our way around it. Betty's neon sign stood out like a shining beacon in the night, and with the tri-pointed form of Mandalay Bay dominating the view out of the windscreen, Las Vegas Boulevard widened to an intimidating eight-lane highway. Through the palm trees the black glass pyramid of Luxor was unmistakable, as was the reclining Sphynx and the 42 billion candela Sky Beam that seared the night sky. Next to this was Excalibur, a Disneyfied idea of a medieval castle but on a massive scale. Also, our hotel for the night, if we could ever find the entrance.

It didn't seem to matter which direction we approached it from, Excalibur's entrance always seemed to be on the other side of a large concrete divider. We'd circled it several times, apparently taking us on a journey from ancient Egypt to New York City via Paris and the tropics, if the view out of the window was anything to go by. Certainly nowhere else would the Statue of Liberty and the Eiffel Tower be found together. Eventually we stumbled across a service road that led towards one of the car parks, and we abandoned the Jeeps to the night before beginning our quest for the check-in desk. This, too, was easier said than done.

In case you were in any doubt, the chief purpose of everything in Las Vegas is to extract as much money from your wallet as possible. Endless psychological research is conducted to establish the best way to lay out a resort's facilities so that cash practically falls out of your pocket as you walk. For example, there are no exits in Vegas; once you're in a casino, every doorway leads only to another opportunity to be parted from your money. There are also very few windows, making it easy to lose track of time while shovelling quarters into a slot machine. Even something as simple as trying to check-in to a hotel is really just another chance to be relieved of a few greenbacks, and between us and the registration desk lay 100,000 square feet of prime gaming real estate and more than 1,200 slot machines. Navigating through this space felt like negotiating the booby-traps in *Indiana Jones and the Temple of Doom*. There was no clear path through the maze and at every turn a strategically placed machine stood before us, beeping and flashing incessantly. Little old ladies who'd succumbed to the Medusa-esque charms of these gaudy obstacles sat in a zombie-like state, endlessly feeding quarters from a giant bucket into the perpetually hungry slot.

If the slots didn't get you, human fly-traps were deployed; we slipped past a bank of machines to be confronted by a raised platform, about which a good-as-naked pole-dancer was gyrating. Groups of balding overweight men were sat around the base of the platform, salivating into their drinks and occasionally flicking dollar bills in the dancer's direction.

Fearing we'd progressed from garish through tacky and into the realms of seedy, I looked across the walk way to see a mother desperately trying to shield her young children from the writhing and twerking before them. I freely admit Vegas was never likely to be my kind of place, but the image of this woman frantically screening her family from a vinyl-clad stripper in what was essentially a hotel lobby, came to symbolise my feelings about the place. I had hoped to find a little Rat Pack cool; instead I was being given back-street Bangkok.

Eventually the sea of slot machines parted to reveal the long-lost check-in desk. Vince completed the registration process with little drama (even his credit card worked) and then it was my turn.

"Welcome to Excalibur," the check-in agent said, rewinding her predefined script to the beginning despite the fact I'd already heard every word. Or so I thought.

"We're very busy this evening I'm afraid..." she began. A feeling of dread washed over me. When a sentence starts like this in a hotel, rarely is there a happy ending.

She continued: "...and I'm afraid the room you reserved is no longer available."

In the words of Scooby Doo: "Ruh-roh."

Was I destined to spend the night in a freezing cold Wrangler? I turned to Vince and gave him a look that was meant to say: "hey there friend, that bare patch of carpet in your room looks mighty comfortable." Thankfully, the agent hadn't finished her spiel.

"So we'll be giving you a complementary upgrade to a higher grade room, at no expense to yourself. I hope that's OK."

Rarely had there been such a turn-around between sentences. From desperation to elation in less than a second.

"Thanks very much!" I replied, turning to Vince who I'd hoped might be pleased at my good fortune. Instead, Vince shot me a look that clearly said just one word:

"Git."

In fact, to this day I don't think Vince has forgiven me.

Clutching our keys, we dragged our bags back through the temple of doom on the quest for our rooms. Excalibur has nearly 4,000 of them arranged in four rectangular towers. My room, with an impossibly high number like 24216, was in a separate tower to Vince's. Having insisted he inspect both rooms, that necessitated mounting an expedition over such a distance as to almost require taking food and water with us. As it turned out, our rooms were exactly the same – except I had a view out on to the strip, while Vince's looked out across a car park.

Vince hasn't forgiven me for having this view out of my hotel room.

After a quick shower, we met up to find somewhere to eat. While Excalibur offers plenty of choices, we preferred to venture out on to the strip to find something a little more interesting. We swung into a few of the big-name casinos to see what each had to offer. Tastes of every conceivable kind were catered for with cuisine from across the world, all served up in a variety of themes. Each property fought with its neighbours to attract their favours, employing everything from replicas of world-famous landmarks to giant illuminated fountains and animatronic displays that rivalled a major theme park. Inside each one, their vast floor space was filled with shops, restaurants, bars and gambling. Their designs varied, from ancient Greece to Jack the Ripper-era London complete with cobbled streets, although the effect was shattered somewhat by the slot machines shoe-horned into every available crevice. We found a venue we liked the look of. Unfortunately Vince was about to ruin his evening.

On the back of the menu was a tantalising selection of cocktails, all with disarmingly innocent names. What the menu didn't make clear was that hidden behind each innocuous title was an alcohol content that would rival jet fuel. Vince ordered a Tutti Fruitti, which duly arrived looking wholesome and angelic, the glass's rim adorned with a variety of fruit, a couple of straws, and the requisite number of umbrellas. Its taste, too, seemed equally harmless, like a sweet blend of fruit juices with the aftertaste of cough syrup. However, as Vince approached the bottom of the glass, his world began to fall apart. Up was down, left was right. All co-ordination disappeared, and he began having trouble staying upright in his seat. Inconceivably, then, he ordered another one. While at the time I can remember thinking this was all quite hilarious, looking back I wish I'd stopped him.

Two sips into his second Tutti Fruitti, the alcohol hit him like an incoming tidal wave. Vince clambered to his feet and, just as he'd done in Eddie McStiff's in Moab, he announced that he needed to go home. Since home was still five thousand miles away, that committed us to negotiating our way through at least two busy casinos purposely designed to stop anyone from leaving, plus whatever dangers awaited us on the streets of Las Vegas. All while distinctly under the influence.

What followed was a high-speed whistle-stop tour of Vegas, mostly consisting of Vince charging off somewhat waywardly into the distance while I tried desperately not to lose him in the crowds of people. Every door that looked like an exit only led into another gaming room, and when we stumbled across a church in the middle of one venue, I felt like sneaking inside to take refuge from it all.

At one point we attracted the attention of a group of rather unsavoury characters who followed us intently through the throngs of people. I can remember putting my hands into my pockets and holding tightly onto my wallet fearing I was about to lose it. When we burst through a set of doors and found ourselves outside on the sidewalk, they thankfully stayed behind.

The cool desert air seemed to have a positive effect on Vince's alcohol-polluted condition and that thankfully meant we made it back to Excalibur without getting run over or mugged. I made sure Vince was pointing roughly in the right direction and entrusted him to the care of the elevator, before I trudged across the casino floor to find my own room somewhere in the opposite tower.

It was gone midnight, but as I weaved through the banks of slot machines and poker tables on my way to bed, Vegas looked like a party that was only just getting started.

CHAPTER SEVENTEEN

Las Vegas to California

05133♫

To BEGIN WITH, I THOUGHT it was a brilliant idea. To save trudging all the way through the casino back to reception, Excalibur's guests can check out from the comfort of their rooms. Although I imagine this has since been replaced by a smartphone app, during our stay it was conducted via a series of menus that appeared on the TV. I'd dutifully followed the prompts on the screen using the remote, and was finally rewarded with the message: "Thank you, check-out complete." Pleased with myself for having avoided a lengthy walk and half a life-time in a queue, my mood changed somewhat when I spotted another message underneath, in writing so small as to be barely discernible: "Check-out fee: $1."

"Typical," I thought to myself. "You even have to pay to leave."

As I dragged my luggage across the road towards the car park, another thought hit me: this was to be our last full day in America. Our target for the day was to reach Laguna Beach in California for our final overnight stay before flying back to England the day after. Before

Vince and John discuss the finer points of suspension articulation while taking shelter underneath this pickup at the Off-Road Expo.

that, however, we'd promised to meet up with a contact in Pomona at the annual Off-Road Expo.

Between Vegas and California lay what should have been four hours of I-15. Predictably, four hours became five, five hours became six. By the time we merged on to I-10 near San Bernardino – another famous Route 66 town – we still had the best part of an hour to go.

California traffic is truly something to behold. I'd seen pictures of twelve lanes of stationary traffic snaking their way along grey concrete freeways, but to some extent I'd always thought it was a myth. That myth was well and truly busted within just a few minutes of joining I-10. With time slipping away from us the sight of a sea of red brake lights made my heart sink.

We inched forward, the Jeeps bobbing over the seams in the concrete like a caged animal unsettled by its surroundings. California's interstates were often rough and uncomfortable and this stretch like many others had been scored deeply, presumably to help dissipate rain water. The Jeeps' mud-terrain tyres howled angrily against the uneven surface, as if complaining at being rubbed by what looked like a giant cheese grater.

We were beginning to attract attention, too. Our two-Jeep convoy drew everything from quizzical glances to kids jumping up and down, pointing. Two 'driver-less' Jeeps aren't something you see on the freeway every day, and although it felt like a lifetime ago, our journey through New York had meant we were by now well used to having our picture taken by a passing motorist.

After seven hours on the road, we finally arrived at the Pomona Fairplex. At more than 543 acres and with over 325,000 square feet of exhibition space, the Fairplex makes other convention centres look like a Saturday market stall. It's been the home of the L.A. County Fair since 1922, but also incorporates an art centre, the RailGiants train museum, and the NHRA Motorsports Museum.

While queueing at the entrance gate, one of the staff wandered over to inspect the Jeeps.

"Why does your exhaust run up the side of the windscreen?" she asked me.

"Oh, that's a snorkel, not an exhaust," I replied. "It's a raised air intake for the engine, rather than an outlet."

A puzzled look swept across her face.

"Why would you need that?"

"It's so you can drive through deep water, or really dusty environments like deserts," I elaborated.

She thought about this for a while, but clearly still wasn't satisfied.

"And having the intake up high helps with that?" she asked.

"Sure. If you drive through water any deeper than this," I explained, marking an imaginary line on the side of the Jeep with my hand, "you risk sucking water into the engine, which will kill it. With the snorkel, you can drive through much deeper water without a problem."

This seemed to make more sense to her, although she was still fascinated by one thing.

"So where does the exhaust go, then?"

"Out the back, just like normal."

"You don't need a snorkel for that?"

"No, exhaust gas comes out of the engine under pressure, so it just forces its way out. Like blowing bubbles in the bath." I was tempted to make a joke about farting, but thought better of it.

Satisfied with my explanation, she started nodding.

"Have you ever had to use it?" she asked.

"Almost had to use it a couple of days ago in Utah," I replied. "They had the worst flooding for a generation, many towns were under several feet of water."

"Wow, that's amazing. You should be alright here," she said. "This is California; hardly ever rains here. Enjoy the Expo!"

She waved us through the gate. In her fascination about the snorkel, she'd apparently been oblivious to the fact the driver she'd been talking to was sitting on completely the wrong side of the Jeep.

The Off-Road Expo had been running for a few years by the time we visited it. Although this year it was sponsored by Toyota, the show brought together manufacturers of all persuasions plus a bewildering array of aftermarket companies all competing for a slice of the growing 4x4 market. Suspension lifts, winches, lights, wheels, tyres, roll cages, trailers, even complete engine swaps were all on display, usually having been fitted to some outlandish show vehicle with a custom paint-job. This seemed to be the year of the giant pickup truck with Dodge Rams and Ford F-250s littering much of the outside display area, each one fitted with vertigo-inducing suspension and oversize tyres. Not surprisingly, it was the Jeeps that interested us the most, and I was continuously drawn to the various Wranglers with 5.7-litre Hemi V8 conversions.

We met up with our contact, John, whose company produces an accessory switch panel, one of which was already installed in the Wrangler. It creates a convenient means of mounting the switchgear for the various off-road goodies such as the diff locks and the winch. John had kindly offered to guide us around the Expo, but had also

If you didn't bring a giant lifted pickup with four-wheel steering and a custom paint-job to the show, you might as well pack up and go home.

wanted the opportunity to take a look at our Jeeps to see if he could improve his design for right-hand-drive vehicles.

John was fascinated by our Jeeps; to him, something so familiar with the steering wheel in the wrong place was just too confusing for words. He insisted we took a few photos of him with both the Wrangler and the Cherokee, and as we did so several other people came over to see what the fuss was about. If Vince and I had been smart, we'd have set-up a stand and charged for photos, such was the interest not only in our Jeeps but also the story of our trip. But with the show now closed and the car park emptying, it was time to say goodbye to John and head on to our hotel.

We joined the Riverside Freeway just outside Corona, a sixteen-lane concrete monster that wound its way around the foothills of the Santa Ana Mountains. Four of the lanes were Express Lanes, accessible only to those who'd paid for the privilege and were separated from the rest

The Laguna Reef Inn, our last (and best) overnight stay.

of the carriageway by unforgiving bollards lined up like ever-vigilant soldiers.

Turning off towards Irvine we left behind the built-up towns and cities as the road wandered through the sun-bleached terrain. Dropping into Laguna Canyon, homes and businesses clung to the hillsides, mirroring the path of the road. It's possible I imagined it, but I felt sure I could feel a more relaxed atmosphere, as if the pace of life had suddenly slowed down a little.

Palm trees, T-shirt shops, and galleries marked our arrival in Laguna Beach. Although the Coast Highway was busy, traffic was still moving freely, calmly, even. Through the gaps between buildings I could just make out the Pacific Ocean beyond as it glinted faintly in the late evening light. With just a mile or so to go to our final hotel, we came across something in the road we'd not seen before in all the miles we'd driven across America.

At the crossroads, the familiar black and white zebra markings of a pedestrian crossing had been painted on the tarmac. There was nothing unusual about that. What was unusual, though, was that accompanying the painted rectangles was a line of orange lights embedded in the road surface. And they were flashing.

Back home in England, when a pedestrian approaches a crossing, traffic must stop to allow them to cross. This didn't seem to be the case here in America, as we'd discovered on our first night in Connecticut when we'd upset the driver of an 18-wheeler by stopping to allow someone to cross. But flashing orange lights leading across the road? We had no idea what that meant. There were no other cars ahead of us from whom to take our lead, but as there didn't appear to be anyone waiting to cross, we gingerly carried on. At least part of me felt that, unlike the cops in Philadelphia, the ones in Laguna Beach were probably too laid back to care about a pair of stupid Brits who didn't know what a flashing pedestrian crossing meant.

Far later than we'd intended, we pulled into the parking lot of the Laguna Reef Inn. The college student behind the reception desk looked surprised to see us, but since I'd pre-paid before leaving England there was little to do but sign-in. We dragged our bags off to our rooms, but even on this brief journey it seemed we'd saved the best hotel 'til last.

The rooms were arranged in two levels around a large courtyard, at the centre of which was a kidney-shaped pool. Sun loungers were laid out at the pool-side awaiting their audience, while beyond this a brick path wound its way between flower beds filled with desert plants, cacti, and bamboo. Several large palms sprouted upwards, towering high above the hotel buildings, lending the courtyard a feeling of being hidden within a sheltered and reassuring jungle.

This comforting feeling extended into the rooms, too. I dumped my bag just inside the door and fell backwards on to the bed. It was like collapsing onto a cloud. So soft and enveloping was it that I struggled to find the motivation to climb back out and head into the shower.

As I rinsed away the stresses of the last few hundred miles, I remembered that this was my last night on American soil. I smiled to myself as some of the trip's memories replayed themselves in my mind.

I couldn't believe this was all ending. Tomorrow would be dominated by packing the Jeeps away ready for their return journey, followed by a frantic rush to the airport.

Everything about that sounded depressing.

CHAPTER EIGHTEEN

California to
London

05424̄ + ✈

V INCE AND I STARTED THE day in a state of denial. There
were a million and one things to attend to, but at that moment
neither of us wanted to be anywhere but in the hotel's
courtyard enjoying a distinctly leisurely breakfast. We both knew all
too well that we were merely delaying the inevitable, but still we were
determined to make our morning last.

Opposite the hotel lay Treasure Island Beach, named after the
Jackie Cooper movie filmed here in 1934. Originally it was a private
beach for a small community, and although now open to the public it's
still considered one for the locals. Access is through an impossibly
idyllic park with sinuous paths, immaculate lawns and intricately
planted borders, none of which would look out of place at the Chelsea
Flower Show. As the path meandered through the park, a selection of
picnic tables, benches, drinking fountains and even showers appeared
in secluded recesses, while raised platforms looked out across the
Pacific Ocean.

I'm not naturally a beach person but even on this somewhat grey and overcast morning, I found the idea of spending time here strangely appealing. I wandered down to the water's edge and, with the sound of the ocean lapping at my toes in the background, I rang home on my cell phone.

"Can you hear that?" I asked, probably at £5 a minute. "That's the Pacific Ocean. We've done it."

At its heart this was a coast-to-coast road-trip, albeit one with the bonus of a few national parks and a fortnight driving off-road across some of the toughest terrain on the planet. Having reached the western-most point of our trip, we should have been celebrating. This was where the line ended when we'd drawn across a map during our prep nine months ago. But since this point also drew our trip to a close, it was difficult not to feel downhearted.

We couldn't hang around to dwell on it, though. Not just because it was costing me a fortune in mobile phone charges, but because ultimately we had a plane to catch.

First, we had to get the Jeeps to a storage facility in Bakersfield, about 180 miles away. Of course we could take the quickest and most direct route along I-5, or we could push our luck and drive a piece of the famous Pacific Coast Highway. Naturally, we chose the latter.

Although officially known by the rather less exciting title of California State Route 1, the PCH runs along the coastline for some 659 miles, reaching from San Diego through Los Angeles and Santa Barbara, over the Big Sur mountains and on to San Francisco via the Golden Gate Bridge. Landslides and coastal erosion have been a constant threat since the first sections were completed in the 1930s, but its immortalisation in cult movies such as *Point Break* has secured its place in many a tourist guide.

Just like Route 66, it's a whole road-trip in its own right, and we could easily have filled our three weeks in America driving just this one road. Instead we had to console ourselves with a 30-mile section through Newport Beach.

While the road often takes a more inland route, obscuring the coastline behind shops and houses, there are places where the ocean's waves appear to almost crash upon the asphalt. At Huntington Beach the interstate is separated from the sand by what appears to be the world's largest car park, while a number of piers jut out into the ocean at several points along our shortened route. Most appeared to be in excellent condition with a thriving retail presence, in stark contrast to the piers in Britain which seem to have an alarming ability to burst into flames and crumble into the sea.

At Seal Beach we finally admitted defeat. We couldn't keep fabricating reasons to string our journey out to the last possible minute. Reluctantly, we turned off the PCH and headed for the interstate.

Our flight left Los Angeles International Airport at 8:50pm. Although at this point we were only 30-odd miles away, we first had to get to Bakersfield - 150 miles north - before double-backing on ourselves to return to LAX. It was mid-afternoon. We would be cutting it extremely fine.

I made a conscious decision not talk to Vince on the radio. I wanted to hunker down and concentrate on counting down the miles, and we picked up the pace as much as we dared. Thankfully traffic on the San Diego Freeway was remarkably well behaved, and we merged on to the I-5 - the Golden State Freeway - just outside San Fernando. Which made me hum Abba songs to myself.

Names of interesting-sounding places flashed by on the satnav's screen - Pyramid Lake, Los Padres National Forest - but with no hope of visiting them. Some, such as Six Flags Magic Mountain could be seen from the freeway, the torturous tracks of its roller-coasters twisting wildly just out of reach. As we cleared the Fort Tejon State Park the undulating terrain gave way to vast open plains and we left the I-5 behind. The plains in turn gave way to vast fields planted with vines and fruit trees in regimented rows that stretched as far as the eye could see. Huge irrigation booms swept across crops so immense they appeared to obscure the horizon. It made me think of Kansas, only fruitier. The crops gave way to houses as we reached the Bakersfield city limits, but also presented something of a logistical challenge: how do two people drive three vehicles?

We left the Wrangler outside the storage facility while Vince and I took the Cherokee to Bakersfield airport to collect our hire car. I'd assumed Bakersfield would be a tiny provincial airfield – in fact its real name is Meadows Field – and this led to me inadvertently upset the lady on the Hertz rental desk.

"This is quite a big terminal building for a small airport," I said, making idle chit-chat while she tapped our details into her computer.

"We're not that small. We handled around 300,000 passengers last year," she replied, with obvious pride.

"Really? That sounds a lot. I thought only small stuff like Cessnas would fly from here," I said, digging myself in further.

"We handle big stuff too, you know." I was probably beginning to grate by this point.

"Like what?" I quizzed.

"We have regular 747 landings here. Plus large cargo aircraft. We're really not that small," she repeated.

I had no idea where I was going with this conversation. All it had achieved so far was to demonstrate my ignorance.

"Well, it's very impressive I must say," I replied, trying to finish on a positive note.

Having always been stung by hire companies' charges, I asked what the refuelling policy was.

"The vehicle should be returned fully fuelled," she replied, although seeing that we were intending to leave it at LAX, she guessed correctly that we might be short of time.

"There is another way," she continued. "The Fuel Purchase Option allows you to buy a tank of gas now at local prices and not have to worry about refuelling at the other end. It usually works out cheaper," she advised.

It was already 5pm and we were running out of time. We'd yet to unload the Jeeps and prep them for storage. We were still 120 miles

The storage depot seemed to go on forever.

from the airport. The last thing we needed to be doing was venturing into downtown LA to look for a gas station.

"Sold," I declared.

She handed me the keys to a car so unimaginative I can't even remember what it was and Vince and I retraced our route back to the storage depot.

It was a brand new facility with pristine concrete and brightly coloured roller shutters. We found our reserved unit part way along a line that seemed to stretch on forever and set about removing anything from the Jeeps that wasn't bolted down. It's not unusual for dock workers to take 'souvenirs' from vehicles as they're loaded on to a ship; a satnav attached to the dashboard in LA almost certainly won't still be there in Southampton. Loose items were restrained or hidden, water was drained out of CamelBaks, and anything that might get a curious shipyard driver into trouble – such as winches and diff-locks – was disabled.

Vince backed the Cherokee into the unit, and then I nosed the Wrangler towards it.

It didn't fit. The unit was about two feet too short. With time running out, we stood back to consider our options. We could rent another unit, but that would be expensive, and there may not be any available. We could try taking the spare wheels off both Jeeps in the hope of making them shorter, but there was no guarantee that would be enough. As we stood there trying to come up with increasingly inventive ways of solving our predicament, a far simpler thought seemed to dawn on us both: just park them at an angle.

Vince performed an elaborate ballet of staccato backwards and forwards motions until the Cherokee was huddled into the far corner of the unit, and then I shunted the Wrangler into the space next to it. Thank God for whoever invented power steering.

With both Jeeps' batteries disconnected, we prepared to leave them behind. But there was no time for long, lingering goodbyes. I patted the Wrangler on the hood, pulled down and locked the roller door, and loaded our bags into the anonymous hire car.

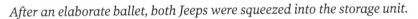

After an elaborate ballet, both Jeeps were squeezed into the storage unit.

After three weeks of being the centre of attention on every freeway, we were now just another bland metal box in a sea of anonymity. One that had only an hour and a half to get to LAX.

P. J. O'Rourke once famously declared that "the fastest car in the world is a rental car." He's not wrong. We had the added bonus of not having to worry about how much fuel was left in ours, and so our anodyne metal box tore its way through the early evening traffic at something approaching light speed. Our heart rates settled a little when the airport exit finally appeared, and we followed the signs to the Hertz drop-off point.

Painted arrows directed us like a trail of breadcrumbs to an open parking area made up of parallel lanes, and here a rather shifty-looking character held up his hand haltingly.

"Just leave it there," he said. "Leave the engine running, I'll take care of it."

I couldn't decide if this was excellent service or he was about to steal our rental right off the lot. He didn't carry any identification, nor was he wearing Hertz-branded clothing. He didn't ask for our details, nor did he want us to sign any paperwork. This all felt rather suspicious to me; if you wanted to steal a car, this would be an ideal place to do it. He was certainly keen to get a move on.

"I'll get the doors, just make sure you've got everything," he demanded as we hurriedly unloaded our belongings from the back of the car. "The terminal bus is about to leave," he announced, piling on the pressure. Check-in was closing, too. We'd run out of time.

We consigned our rental car to the care of the random man in the car park and sprinted towards the bus. As I jumped aboard the bus driver closed the doors behind me, crushing my bag between them. I didn't realise what had happened at first; I tried to step further into the bus but for some reason my bag had become incredibly heavy.

"Hey, would you mind opening the doors, I'm trapped," I asked the driver as he started to pull away.

"Sure, no problem," he replied calmly, as if his bus eating a passenger were an everyday occurrence. The doors opened and my bag was released from their custody, the bus accelerating towards the terminal all the while.

"Where y'all headed?" the driver shouted over the din of the engine.

Vince and I were in semi-panic mode and concentrating on getting through the airport as quickly as possible; we weren't ready for a conversation. We glanced around at the other passengers, but no-one else answered.

"We're heading back to London," Vince replied.

We'd been rushing about all day. But as hostages of the terminal transfer bus, there was little we could do but take a moment to draw breath. If that meant having a conversation with the driver, so be it, although the enforced calmness of it felt more than a little surreal.

"Been in America long?" the driver asked.

"About three weeks." Vince took up the narrative. "We did a coast-to-coast road-trip." It seemed strange to hear Vince talk about it in the past tense for the first time.

"America's great for road-trips," the driver shouted over the banging and crashing as the bus rattled its way towards the terminal building.

"Yes... yes it is," I thought to myself.

"Which airline?" the driver asked as the terminal came into view.

"Virgin, but we're a little late. If you could point us in the right direction that would be great," we replied.

"I can do better. I'll drop you right outside."

We shouted our thanks as we jumped off the bus and ran into the terminal, dragging our reluctant bags behind us. It seems LAX is far kinder to its passengers than JFK and the check-in desk was right where the unmissable giant sign said it would be. We lunged at the check-in agent, tickets and passports in hand. She looked at them briefly.

"Just in time," she announced. The relief hit me, and my pulse rate began to return to normal. Perhaps taking pity on our somewhat frazzled appearance, she slid two passes to the Virgin lounge across the counter towards us.

"Gate 26, but you've got some time to relax first," she said with a wry smile.

The frosted glass doors glided open silently as we approached and I suddenly felt incredibly underdressed. In a world of expensive suits and designer casualwear, my boots, grubby T-shirt and cargo trousers made me look like I'd just fallen out of a tractor.

Vince and I retired to a pair of colourful tub chairs in a quiet corner and my mind succumbed to reverie – Vince staggering through Vegas, the scale of Hoover dam, baked bean pizza, everything about Colorado, driving through a tornado, coffee-soaked pancakes, our near-arrest in Philadelphia.

But it was also the people we'd met that had made this trip what it was. From the human refrigerator I'd met in a Connecticut gas station to the proprietor of the St. Elmo General Store; the staff of the Jeep dealership in Indiana to the waitresses of many a Denny's with their ready smile and warm welcome, even at 2am.

Driving two British Jeeps hadn't just allowed us to use our own vehicles on some of the finest off-road trails this country has to offer. They'd been giant four-wheeled ice-breakers, a way to meet more people and see further into a country than we'd ever have been able to from the seat of some anonymous rental car.

And what a country.

We may have driven 5,500 miles across 15 states, but there was still so much that we'd missed. Our itinerary punished us from the moment we landed and didn't let up until we arrived in this lounge. What we needed was more time.

I looked across at Vince who wore an expression that suggested he was lost in similar thoughts.

"Vince, the federal exemption on our Jeeps lasts for a year, doesn't it?" I asked him.

"It does."

I paused for a moment.

"You know, instead of shipping them back, we could just leave them here," I suggested cagily. "Just for a few months. They're quite safe in storage."

Vince sat upright in his chair.

"And then fly back in a few months and pick them up?" Vince asked, clearly already following my chain of thought.

"Yes. And then do it all again," I continued.

Vince smiled at the idea. "All of it?"

"Well... maybe not so many miles in a day next time."

*

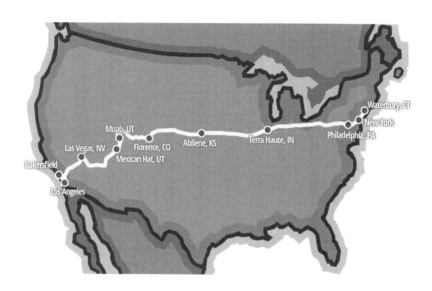

For bonus content including photos, maps and exclusive information about this trip, visit the Two Jeeps website:

www.twojeeps.com

ABOUT THE AUTHOR

Alex Kefford is a freelance journalist writing mainly in the automotive and technology fields. He's also an experienced off-roader and instructor, and as the founder of JeepClub he's spent many a weekend teaching driving techniques to those new to Jeep ownership. His love of America has led him to believe he was born in the wrong country.

Made in the USA
Columbia, SC
02 November 2021

48272003R00115